Concord
AND
Liberty

by JOSÉ ORTEGA Y GASSET

JOSÉ ORTEGA Y GASSET

Concord

AND

Liberty

Translated from the Spanish by HELENE WEYL

The Norton Library

W · W · NORTON & COMPANY · INC ·

NEW YORK

Contents

Translator's Preface

OF THE FOUR essays that compose this volume three were written and first published in Argentina during the author's exile from his native Spain.

Concord and Liberty, which bears the Spanish title *Del imperio romano*, was published as a series of articles in the Sunday supplement of the Buenos Aires newspaper *La Nación* in the summer of 1940. Together with the author's essay *History as a System* it forms a booklet published by Revista de Occidente in 1941.

Notes on Thinking—Its Creation of the World and Its Creation of God opens the first issue (1941) of the Argentine philosophical journal *Logos*, which is published by the Facultad de Filosofía y Letras of the University of Buenos Aires. The original title of the essay is *Apuntes sobre el pensamiento—su demiurgia y su teurgia*.

Prologue to a History of Philosophy was written as a preface to the Spanish translation of Émile Bréhier's *History of Philosophy*, Editorial Sudamericana, 1942. Under the title *Prólogo a una filosofía* it forms one of the two essays of the book *Dos prólogos*, Revista de Occidente, 1944.

A Chapter from the History of Ideas—Wilhelm Dilthey and the Idea of Life was first published in the Spanish literary journal *Revista de Occidente*, November, December, 1933, and January, 1934, on the occasion of Dilthey's one hundredth anniversary under the title *Guillermo Dilthey y la idea de la vida* and later included in the book *Teoría de Andalucía y otros ensayos*, Revista de Occidente, 1944.

The change of title in the first essay must seem bold. The

justification, which the translator is anxious to give, applies not only to this but also to a few other less conspicuous changes. All Ortega's writings are parts of a continuous imaginary dialogue between the author and his Spanish-speaking audience. They are, on the whole, independent and well-rounded parts. But occasionally reference is being made in them to further communications which then fail to materialize. The essay *Del imperio romano* was to be a series of fireside talks on the political structure of the Roman Empire. The conversations came to an untimely end. But what we have of them forms, after a few minor changes, a profound and comprehensive lecture on a problem that certainly is of general interest.

I wish to use this opportunity for thanking my friend M. D. Herter Norton, whose fine and honest hands have helped to mend many of the smaller mistakes that are apt to mar the style of one writing in a language not entirely her own.

Concord
AND
Liberty

Contents

INTRODUCTION

PROFESSOR ROSTOVTZEFF'S great book on the social and economic history of the Roman Empire [1] made an unwonted stir in the small circles of those alive to historical problems. And it did so for good reasons. The history of Rome, by virtue of its content and of the comprehensiveness of our knowledge of it, may well be called a model history. But for us this exemplary history ended where Mommsen left it, with Julius Caesar. What comes after, the Empire, remained little more than a legend. Yet those centuries, in the course of which the Occident was latinized, in which it took over and evolved, once and for all, fundamental ways of feeling and thinking, witness the entrance on the historical scene of what is to be Europe. The history of the Empire, unlike that of the Republic and of Greece, is not a predecessor of European history; it marks its first stage.

But Rostovtzeff's work has not only been acclaimed by scholars—the pitiable shadows scholars are in these days; his book also contrives to be of undeniable actuality, provided actuality is taken at more than its surface meaning. Nor is it by chance that the remote centuries of imperial Rome are stirring again in our time, and that a subject chosen by the curious intelligence of a historian shows striking analogies to the present state of the world. Great books are no windfall. Rather the opposite: Mommsen, who was a historian of herculean power, came to a halt on the threshold of the Empire because his political experiences and those of his time ended there. Nineteenth-century understanding did not reach beyond the Republic, beyond Rome in the ascendant, Rome with her faith in herself and her gods

[1] M. I. Rostovtzeff, *The Social and Economic History of the Roman Empire*, Oxford, Clarendon Press, 1941.

unshaken, living by a "deep-rooted concord" and by what was felt to be "freedom."

But it was through the vanishing of "concord" and "liberty" —two things at once ethereal and most substantial—that the form of life called Roman Empire came into being. The two terms are taken from Cicero, who uses them to express the anxiety with which he watched the changing aspect of life about him. This aspect coincides in some of its essential features with the turn our own existence has been taking during the last thirty years. A new historical scenery, profoundly different from that which hitherto has served as background for the adult life of the Western nations, is coming into view. And suddenly illuminated by the light of the new historical day, those remote centuries of imperial Rome stand out in bold relief before the eye of the historian. No, Rostovtzeff's work has not happened to coincide with actual developments; it has been inspired by them.

Concordia, libertas! I know of no attempt to ascertain the *authentic* meaning Cicero connected with the two words— that is, the meaning he experienced when he wrote or said them. Thus an exegesis of the two terms may provide an appropriate basis for the present investigation.

DICTIONARY AND CIRCUMSTANCE

Nobody will make bold to maintain that the meaning of a word can be gathered from dictionaries. A dictionary furnishes, at best, a general scheme in which the manifold actual significations a word admits of may be inserted. But the real meaning of a word appears when the word is uttered and functions in the human activity called speech. Hence we must know who says it to whom, when and where. Which indicates that meaning, like all things human, depends on circumstance. In the operation of speaking—that is, communicating through words—what we call language forms only one, if a relatively stable, constituent which must be supplemented by the vital setting.

For an illustration let us consider what a lot of different things the word "black" may suggest—so many, in fact, that the mind remains blank for mere *embarras de choix*. Even to think of a color is not absolutely necessary, as there are also black moods. But when the guest says "black," the hostess knows that he takes no cream in his coffee. What the word fails to say, circumstance mutely adds. Language is a text that calls for illustrations. The illustrations are furnished by the lived and living reality out of which a man speaks, a reality essentially unstable and fleeting, emerging and vanishing never to return. The real meaning of a word is not in the dictionary; it is in the instant. After twenty-five centuries of mental training to grasp reality *sub specie aeterni*, we must make a new start and develop an intellectual technique for detecting it *sub specie instantis*.

CONCORDIA

REASON AND VICISSITUDE

It was in the midst of a civil war that Cicero wrote his book *De Republica* (On the State). Nor did he for one moment mistake the ominous difference between the political crises that had been shaking Rome for twenty years and the numerous conflicts his country had passed through before. This was not one of those struggles that may occur in any normal course of political life when the social body, thrown out of balance through its own growth, briefly readjusts itself. One of Cicero's purposes in writing his treatise was precisely to set forth a great idea which he had learned, though he does not say so, from Polybius, that most penetrating of ancient historians, or philosophers of history if one so prefers.

Polybius came into touch with Rome when she was about to expand her reign over the whole basin of the Mediterranean, thus for the first time joining the Orient with the Occident. A political power of such nature surpassed all previous historical experiences of mankind. With a perspicacity perhaps unique in the length and breadth of historical thinking, Polybius, the great Greek from Megalopolis, was fully aware of the destiny in store for this commonwealth and of the peculiar structure of its state. In his *History* we read at the end of the second fragment of Book VI:

Lykurgus, then, foreseeing by a process of reasoning whence and how events naturally happen, constructed his constitution untaught by adversity. But the Romans, while they have arrived at the same final result as regards their form of government, have not reached it by any process of reasoning but by the discipline of vicissitudes. And always choosing the best by the light of experience gained in disaster, they have reached the same result as Lykurgus, that is to say, the best of all existing constitutions.

Reason and vicissitude—no minor theme indeed for a meditation on our time, to confront these two formidable historical powers and let them argue their cases against each other. At bottom they are but two forms of reason: the one pure reason which "starts from concepts, proceeds by concepts and terminates in concepts"—thus Plato defines dialectics—the other historical reason which arises fulminantly from the nature of things.

The quoted passage from Polybius shines through at various places in Cicero's lucubrations on the state. Thus in *De Republica* II, 33, where he says that "after the establishment of the Republic the people, freed from the domination of the kings, claimed a somewhat greater measure of right" and then proceeds: "This claim may have meant a lack of reason; but the very nature of public questions frequently overpowers reason—*vincit ipsa rerum publicarum natura saepe rationem.*"

Cicero was as clearly aware of this interplay of reason and experience as he was of the other point implied in Polybius' sentence: that vicissitudes or political struggles are not necessarily negative events, indicative of social disease, but on the contrary may help to bring forth a better state. "When there is mutual fear, man fearing man and class fearing class—*ordo ordinem*—then, because no one is confident of his own strength, a sort of bargain is made between the common people and the mighty; this results in that mixed form of government which Scipio has been recommending" [2]—namely, the combination of monarchy, aristocracy, and democracy. The passage could not be more nineteenth century, since it literally speaks of class struggle and the constitutional pact.

Far from extolling internal peace or regarding public life as a matter of suave urbanity, Cicero held *dissensiones civiles* to be the very condition on which the welfare of the state is based and from which it derives. If the events he witnessed terrified him, we may therefore be sure that it was not simply because they were fraught with strife and conflict. Unfortunately the beginning of Book VI of *De Republica* in which Cicero must have advanced his concept of civil dissension has particularly suffered from time and weather. The scattered fragments allow us to conjecture that in his analysis Cicero referred to the revolutions of the city as being caused by civil discord. This gap we now propose to fill with a construction of our own—an attempt to understand Cicero's mind by evoking his circumstances.

STRATA OF DISCORD

Intestine strife, Cicero had read in Aristotle, arises when the members of a society disagree about public matters—a somewhat hackneyed statement. However, have we not just seen that discord may also give the impulse for further development and perfection of the state? On the other hand, a society obviously relies for its existence upon common consent in certain ultimate matters. Such unanimity Cicero calls *concordia,* and he defines it as "the best bond of permanent union in any commonwealth." [3] How does the one tally with the other? Quite

[2] *De Republica* III, 13.
[3] *Ibid.,* II, 42.

easily, if we picture the body of opinions from which the life of
a nation draws its sustenance as made up of various layers.
Divergencies in surface layers produce beneficent conflicts because the ensuing struggles move upon the firm ground of
deeper concord. Questioning certain things but not questioning
all, minor divergencies serve but to confirm and consolidate the
underlying unanimity of the collective existence.

But if dissent affects the basic layers of common belief on
which the solidarity of the social body lastly rests, then the state
becomes a house divided, society dis-sociates, splitting up into
two societies—that is, two groups with fundamentally divergent
beliefs. As there is no room for two societies within one social
space, radical dissension necessarily terminates in the annihilation of the society in which it befalls.

And such precisely was the turn events were taking in the
lifetime of Cicero's generation. What he beheld was not merely
a struggle, if an uncommonly violent one, *within* the human
setting that from time immemorial had been the Roman commonwealth, but the total destruction of that community. The
state of mind accompanying such a situation has little to do with
the motives underlying surface disagreements. These the citizen
fights out with zest, nay with gusto. His adversary is not his
deadly foe; friendship endures beneath hostility. "A contest
between friends, not a quarrel between enemies, is called a disagreement—*benivolentium concertatio, non lis inimicorum iur-
gium dicitur.*" [4] Above the contending parties there persist in
full validity certain common circumstances to which they both
can resort. These are dogmas about life and the universe, moral
norms, legal principles, rules regulating the very forms of the
struggle. Thus both sides feel that in their fight they are securely
held and equally protected by one familiar world. While they
fight, state and society stand firm around them.

But when all this has crumbled, when the state lies in ruins,
when laws, norms, ideas have gone down with it, when parties

[4] *Ibid.,* IV, 8.

find no common ground on which to meet—then a man may feel that he witnesses "the decay and dissolution of the whole universe—*si omnis hic mundus intereat et concidat.*" [5] And are not we now staggering under the impact of this same experience?

CONCORD AND BELIEF

Cicero was not the first to mourn the loss of concord. The idea of concord as the groundwork of society had been hackneyed since Aristotle. One of his disciples, Dicaearchus, wrote a treatise on concord which has not come down to us. And in the fourth century B.C. some Greek states, Heraclea for instance, kept magistrates with the name of *ephoros tes homonoias,* inspector of unanimity. Many a time have I mused over this suggestive title, and though I detest holding office, this I should have been eager to attend to.

Like all educated Romans—indeed like ourselves two thousand years later—Cicero was content to express whatever he saw or suffered in terms of Greek philosophy. The discrepancy between the coined terms—which he used and which we are using—and the realities they refer to is not harmful once it is noticed; only care must be taken always to close the gap between the two lest we complain about one thing while it is another that irks us. "My love," writes Heine, "I have a toothache in my heart." Thus Cicero saw his world becoming a shambles and he cried out: "Concord is lacking"—as people might have cried out one hundred, two hundred, three hundred years before him. But the discord of his time was profoundly different from that of previous ages; it seemed, and it was, irreparable. Cicero felt and sensed the crisis, and in using the word *concordia* or its opposite *dissensio* he knew full well that it was something else he wanted to express. Meanwhile he used the hoary vocables with new connotations and mental reservations—as when we tell ourselves: "Indeed, this is not what I

[5] *Ibid.,* III, 23.

mean, but I can understand myself." And do we not all in writing and talking find out in the end that none but we understand ourselves?

To move on his own in the intellectual medium was not given to Cicero. Where Greek thinking ended, his thinking ended, too. And as regards the question of concord, Aristotle had not quite succeeded in bagging the hare. In the *Nicomachean Ethics* he says that "of political concord we may only speak if the citizens agree in matters concerning the state—that is, if in this respect they pursue the same ends." This may sound convincing enough; yet Aristotle is right only in so far as he lets the hare escape. To begin with, his definition does not furnish a yardstick by which to gauge the degree of agreement or disagreement. Opinion on certain political points may remain split after unanimity has been attained on others of more importance. Discord, like concord, can assume fundamental and ultimate character only if the point in question is itself of fundamental and ultimate import in the life of the state. But an issue of such weight cannot be raised by a mere political incident. With his first example, Aristotle—himself unaware of it—puts us on the right track. "For instance," he writes, "when all citizens agree that magistrates must be elected." Ah yes, this is a matter of great moment. How momentous, indeed, will at once be revealed when we give it its general and rightful name, calling it agreement as to who shall rule. "The function of ruling and obeying is the decisive one in every society. As long as no unanimity obtains about this, everything else, down to the private life of each individual, will drag along in a clumsy and confused fashion." [6]

Thus *concord in its pure and radical form implies a firm and common belief regarding the exercise of supreme power.* Belief —in my terminology this word is pregnant with a whole powerful and precise theory, of which, however, I can here treat only briefly. A belief must be distinguished from an accepted idea, a scientific truth, for instance. Ideas are open to discussion; they

[6] Cf. the author's book *The Revolt of the Masses*, New York, W. W. Norton and Co., 1932, p. 152.

convince by virtue of reason; whereas a belief can neither be challenged nor, strictly speaking, defended. While we hold a belief, it constitutes the very reality in which we live and move and have our being.

A belief in the strict sense of my terminology is unlikely to occur as belief of individuals or particular groups. Since it is not a mere opinion, an idea, a theory, it will normally be of a collective nature. People are inclined to believe in company and not of their own accord. A belief functions when established in a social environment by virtue of its "collective validity"— that is, regardless of the adherence of individual persons or groups. When we find that a conviction depends for its influence in the community upon the willingness of people to fight and die for it, we may be sure that this conviction is in the process either of establishing itself or of ceasing to exist as an actually operative belief. Such conviction may be an inspiring idea which exalts the life of its followers; but it does not create concord. On the contrary, convictions of a group are prone to foment revolution.

This is a matter not to be trifled with. Concord, that kind of concord which forms the foundation of stable society, presupposes that the community holds a firm and common, unquestionable and practically unquestioned, belief as to the exercise of supreme power. And that is tremendous. For a society without such a belief has little chance of obtaining stability. Ideas, even great ones, may be improvised; not so beliefs. Beliefs, to be sure, begin as ideas. But in the process of slowly pervading the minds of the multitude they lose the character of ideas and establish themselves as "unquestionable realities."

A belief, moreover, in a matter so intricate and stirring as the problem of rule cannot exist of itself. It must derive from more fundamental beliefs concerning human life and the reality of the universe. Here we come upon the second weak point in the Aristotelian definition of concord. Political unanimity implies more than an agreement on politics. However secondary political questions by themselves may be, they can be resolved only if agreement prevails in nonpolitical matters, agreement which, in the last instance, concerns the reality of the world.

Each of the European nations lived for centuries in a state of unity because they all believed blindly—all belief is blind—that kings ruled "by the grace of God." To hold such a belief they clearly had to believe in the existence of God. Which meant that they felt they lived not by themselves, alone with their man-made ideas, but in the ceaseless presence of an absolute entity—God—with which they had to reckon. This indeed is belief: to reckon with an inescapable presence. And this is reality: that which must be reckoned with, whether we like it or not. When the peoples of Europe lost the belief, the kings lost the grace, and they were swept away by the gusts of revolution.

Our time stands in need of a new revelation. A revelation obtains whenever man comes into touch with a reality distinct from himself. It does not matter what this reality is made of, provided man feels it to be absolute reality and not his idea, not presumptive or imaginary reality. Man needs a new revelation. For he will be lost in the arbitrary and boundless fancies of his mind if he is not able to contrast them with something truly and inescapably real. Reality is the only mentor and master of man. Without its inexorable and solemn presence it is idle to hope for culture, civil welfare, or even—and that is the most dreadful—authenticity in personal life.

When this reality, the one and only power that checks and disciplines man from within, vanishes because belief in it is slackening, the social domain falls prey to passions. The ensuing vacuum is filled by the gas of emotion. Everyone proclaims what best suits his interest, his whims, his intellectual manias. To escape the void and the perplexities of his own soul, a man will rush to join any party standard that is being carried through the streets. With society gone there remain only parties.

Cicero knew full well that the classes that could be drawn upon for political office in Rome in his time believed in neither the institutions nor the gods of Rome. Regarding the last he needed to consult nobody. He, a priest, had no faith himself. In his book *De Natura Deorum* (Concerning the Nature of the Gods)—the most amazing work ever written by a priest—he scans the whole universe in search of his lost gods.

AUSPICES, OR RELIGION AND NEGLIGENCE

Nonetheless, Cicero made a last attempt to rouse the conscience of his countrymen; he wrote his book on the state upon which we are here commenting. Evoking the shadow of the greatest of all Romans, Scipio Aemilianus, who in his turn evokes the still more venerable shadow of the other Scipio, the elder Africanus, he sets forth, in what may be called a phantasmagoric foreshortening of the history of Rome, the sublime architecture of those institutions which had brought about the triumph of the city without equal. In this review of the events that through the centuries had been shaping the Roman constitution, Cicero leads up to a point where he declares that all achievements thus attained are secondary in comparison with the initial feat of Romulus, who established "those two excellent foundations of our commonwealth, the auspices and the senate." [7] Nothing else and in this order. The senate was the central institution of Rome, on whose right to rule no doubt had ever been cast up to the great civil war in which Cicero wrote. What surprises us is to hear the auspices mentioned as something even more important than the senate, as the core of the core of Roman history.

Like it or no, we are the grandsons or great-grandsons of M. Homais; and we cannot help being slightly amused by the sight of Roman magistrates consulting the auspices and concerning themselves, in unmitigated earnest, about the flight, appetite, and song of birds. Yet our contempt is but a form of stupidity. In fact, the utter ingenuousness of those rites only serves to disclose the more clearly the source whence they draw their inspiration. In consulting auspices, man recognizes that

[7] *De Republica* II, 10.

he is not alone, that around him somewhere are absolute realities more potent than he with which he must reckon. Instead of plunging forthright into such actions as his mind may suggest, he ought to pause and submit his project to the judgment of the gods. Whether such judgment reveals itself in the flight of birds or in the reflections of the prudent is of lesser concern; what matters is that man is taking into account something that transcends him. To live not wantonly but warily—wary of a transcendental reality—is the strict meaning of the Latin word *religiosus,* and indeed the essential meaning of all religion. What a man believes, and what he therefore regards as unquestionable reality, constitutes his religion. *Religio* does not derive from *religare,* to bind—that is, man to God. The adjective, as is often the case, has preserved the original meaning of the noun, and *religiosus* stands for scrupulous, not trifling, conscientious. The opposite of religion thus would be negligence, carelessness, indifference, laxity. Over against *re-ligo* we have *nec-lego; religens (religiosus)* is contrasted with *neglegens.*[8]

In Cicero's opinion the auspices, because they embodied the firm and common belief about the universe on which Roman concord rested, had to be regarded as one of the main factors in bringing about the great centuries of the Republic. So close was the connection between auspices and state that *auspicium* came to be synonymous with *imperium,* rule. To be under the auspices of someone meant to be at his order. And vice versa, the word *augurium* (etymon to the French *mal-heur, bon-heur*), which originally denoted only increase, growth, enterprise, and from which derive *auctoritas* and *augustus,* came to be mixed up with *auspicium* and to designate presage, omen. A fusion took place between the concepts of state and of belief. In politics, there are epochs of religion and epochs of negligence, of care and of carelessness, of probity and of frivolity.

What then happens in a society—and what in particular happened in Rome—after the loss of a firm and common belief in matters of leadership? Society automatically requires the execu-

[8] Aulus Gellius, *Noctium atticarum libri XX* IV, 9.

tive function. Lacking a true solution to the problem of ruling, a makeshift has to be resorted to.

Cicero had a project of a sort in which he himself did not place much confidence; he advanced it in his book on the state. This project of Cicero's was soon to be realized, without mention of Cicero, to be sure, by Augustus who killed Cicero. The project was—the Roman Empire, a makeshift, the most illustrious makeshift in history.

LIBERTAS

UTOPIAN SOCIETY

Cicero knew that what he witnessed was the death agony not only of Roman unity but also of Roman liberty. In his books and letters of the last epoch the word *libertas*, like an obstinate phantom shrouded in mournful nostalgia, looms up on every page. It is his farewell salute to a whole way of life, not his personal life alone but the life of his country as well. This subjective, emotional, and ultimate meaning which the word *libertas* held for him, the meaning, therefore, which he wanted to express by it, we are now anxious to grasp.

First of all we must try to forget whatever the nineteenth century used to connect with the word. Cicero's *libertas* must not be confounded with the liberty or the liberties of liberalism. To begin with, the claim of liberalism to have first discovered and propagated freedom seems hardly justified. The truth is that freedom has been the normal condition of life throughout European, in contrast to Oriental, history. Whoever has been concerned in a somewhat serious fashion with the past of the Western world must have found ample evidence of this. If the reader wants proofs, he need not go to any scholarly exertion; it will do to read a lucid, short, and representative book like Guizot's *Histoire de la civilization Européenne*, a course of lectures delivered in 1820 when the author was still quite young. Guizot could not draw upon more recent investigations, mainly of the last fifty years, which have shown that such events in European history as bear illiberal or antiliberal features can be explained either as adventitious social phenomena, which could not be helped and were soon set right, or as residues of the Roman Empire, which it naturally took a long time to eliminate—serfdom for instance.

Another questionable point in the doctrine of modern liberalism seems to me its belief that society is a good thing that works with the neat precision of a Swiss watch. We are now paying with grim sufferings for this mistake of our forebears and for the complacency with which they gloried in a noble and irresponsible liberalism. Nor will public life throughout the world be in any better way until it has dawned upon us that society is not a nice thing, that it is a terrible thing. Representing, no doubt, the indispensable condition for man's being truly man, society is at the same time his veriest hell. I do not know if there is a hell beyond the confines of this world; but I do know that there is one right among us: society. It captivates us with the delights it offers, only to torture us all the more cruelly.

The very name "society" as denoting groups of men who live together is equivocal and utopian. According to the customary definition, societies exist thanks to man's sociable or social nature—a definition worthy of Molière's Bachelierus. If it is, nonetheless, accepted, on the ground that without a dose of sociability human coexistence is obviously unthinkable, any sociology must at least make all haste to state with equal emphasis, and *to accord equal weight to,* the fact that man is also unsociable and bristling with antisocial impulses. Both social and antisocial forces are at work wherever men are living together. In view of this, does it not mean garbling the facts and barring, from the outset, the way to a true understanding of the eternal tragedy that is human coexistence, when such a reality is simply called "society"? Why omit in the name the antisocial component? By simply inserting it we shall become aware that no society has ever been a "society." Men, to be sure, live together, but their living together cannot truly be called a society. It merely is an attempt or an effort toward becoming one, if it is not an outright wasting away of earlier relatively accomplished forms of social organization. Society, by its own nature, provides the place for social and antisocial doings alike, crime occurring as normally as love of one's neighbor. Major criminal elements may at best be kept at bay temporarily. But even so they only lie concealed in the underworld of the social body ready at any moment to break loose *de profundis.*

Let it not even be said, therefore, that society means the triumph of the social over the antisocial forces. Such triumph has never come to pass. What in fact prevails is an unceasing fight between the two forces, and the ups and downs characteristic of all struggle. When speaking of a satisfactory condition or a good period in the evolution of this or that society, we must keep in mind that such qualification is relative. Nothing social has ever been good in the sense in which a picture, an idea, a character, or an action is good. So reconciled to this fact have people come to be that they will call a policy excellent if it happens not to be the very worst; just as Socrates in prison was delighted when the shackles were removed from his ankles. While we should therefore think that every precaution and vigilance are needed to let social ways and forces prevail over antisocial tendencies, liberalism proclaimed the principle of laissez faire, and liberal politicians were careful to interfere as little as possible.

Society does not work miraculously by itself like a healthy organism. If it works—and so it does; not always, but in most cases—it certainly works not miraculously or spontaneously, as liberalism would have it, but lamentably, owing to the fact that the best parts of the positively social elements let themselves be consumed in the sad pursuit of imposing order upon the antisocial remainder of the so-called society. This pursuit—horrible for many reasons, but indispensable—thanks to which human coexistence turns into *something like* a society, is called rule, and its apparatus is the state. In his book *De legibus* Cicero enunciates solemnly that "without government existence is impossible for a household, a city, a people, the human race, physical nature and the universe itself." [9] But government and consequently the state, in the last instance, spell violence, mitigated in prosperous times, formidable in times of crisis.

Liberalism has never been quite capable of grasping the significance of the fierce nature of the state, that congenital prerequisite of society. Hegel, at the opposite pole, deified the state in an absurd mysticism. Why not comply with the prime duty of intelligence and accept things as they are without additions or subtractions? Let us admit that societies cannot exist without government and state authority; that government implies force (and other things, more objectionable but which it would take too long to enumerate); and that for this reason "participation in government is fundamentally degrading," as Auguste Comte, *whose political theory was authoritarian,* said in an amazing sentence which, dropped casually at an inconspicuous place, has escaped notice. A weird thing indeed this reality we call society, in which the socially most valuable elements are obliged to devote themselves to a degrading task and to prove, by accepting this obligation, their superior sense of responsibility. The recognition of this fundamental fact will have to stand at the beginning of any future sociology. Our inherited ideas about society obviously serve us no longer. We must get rid of them and look again with new eyes, bright and untender, at the things themselves.

With all this *ex abrupto* I know I have been far from saying what ought to be said on liberalism. Liberalism has passed away without ever receiving a proper obituary; and yet its doctrines, as will appear in the course of this investigation, contain more than one strong point. But our purpose here is different, and we must return to it.

[9] *De legibus* III, 1.

LIBERTAS AND LIBERTIES

Roman liberty is an indivisible whole, existing in the singular, as it were, whereas in liberalism liberty appears broken up into a plurality of liberties which, outgrowing all historical dimensions, assume the character of theological entities. This conception that a man is politically free if he can act according to his own will in certain definite dimensions of life is open to discussion. There is, in principle, no single liberty man cannot forgo and yet feel as free as ever.

The best instance of what I wish to indicate may be found in a rather undramatic freedom which was, however, chronologically the first to be emphasized by liberalism at the end of the eighteenth century, which furnished the pattern for subsequent liberties, and which gave the impulse for setting down the liberal doctrine. For it is a fact, and we must not garble facts, that liberalism began with advocating free trade.

Around 1800 the European economy had reached a point where capitalism felt capable of maximum expansion. Capitalism is the economy of production and as such admits of a virtually unlimited production, which in its turn calls for a market that is also unlimited. Such a practically infinite market lay before those nations that were the first to develop great industries. So long as they could count on an indefinitely growing market, the producers did not seriously get into each other's way. Hence no inconvenience arose from their operating with perfect freedom. But after a few decades the situation had changed.

In my opinion, the progressive reduction of economic liberty is not so much due to the restrictions that labor has compelled the state to impose upon producers as to the intrinsic, spontaneous evolution of capitalism itself, which has built up industries (including the new forms of agriculture) in certain quarters of the globe that before had been only markets. The market has thus ceased to be unlimited. Its total volume is still expanding; but as production grows faster it presses upon the market, and thus producers, being faced with a relatively shrinking market capacity, cannot help interfering with each other. Economic freedom becomes impossible—impossible not because of the other fellow's hostile intentions, but because of the material conditions inherent in the situation itself.

In fine, the situation is the same as in urban traffic. Even in times of most unmitigated tyranny European man was free to move through the streets as he pleased, at least before curfew. Modern city administrations have deprived him of this freedom. An official with a magic whistle and hieratic gestures now controls his movements at street corners. The reader would not smile quite so indulgently if he knew a little about the history of human traffic rules—the anxieties and struggles they caused —and if I had time to draw for him a map of the rigidly defined paths along which an African Bantu of a certain age, sex, and rank is, up to this very day, allowed to travel between the fourteen huts of his native village.

My thesis is this: that there is no single concrete liberty which circumstances may not some day make impossible; but the abolishment of a liberty for material reasons does not give us a sense of being curtailed in our free condition. Some of the liberties that the nineteenth century set such store by may quietly be forgone in the course of time, while dimensions of life in which we are still unfree may enter the zone of freedom. Human freedom—and we speak of political freedom only—is not dependent on the materialization of any one form of freedom. Liberal constitutions themselves implicitly admit this in providing for possible suspension of all liberties under special—that is, transitorial—circumstances. But circumstances that are accidental in certain periods can be the rule in others.

KINGS, THE ROCK OF LAW, AND A FEW MANIAS

To Cicero as to any Roman, the word *libertas* in its political sense conveyed one very precise, if exclusively negative, meaning: that of "public life without kings." For various reasons we find ourselves at a loss to understand a Roman's innate aversion to royalty. Europe has lived for the best part of her history under the rule of crowned heads. She is indebted to them for a few hours of happiness; and when she decided to discard them, she went about it without ire, as though removing to the attic an obsolete piece of furniture. Even France though she hated other things, a lot of things—the French Revolution was the heyday of resentment—even France can scarcely be said to have hated her benign Louis XVI.

Rome, however, preserved her dislike of kings surprisingly intact throughout the centuries. Strictly speaking, she never lost it down to her last hour, and this recoiling from royalty is one of the most constant components of the extraordinary form of government that was the Empire.

The roots of so fervid an antimonarchism are multiple. The strongest is doubtless marked by that nation's strange passion for the law. We readily understand that a nation may be fascinated by power, wealth, pleasure, even science, as was Athens. But that a people should set its heart on law of all things seems odd, at least to us—though perhaps only because we fail to comprehend the true meaning of law. How can we, born into a time that has minced law with the extrajuridical chopper of justice and that holds that law is law because it is just, whereas for the Roman the law was just because it was the law.

Law is born from despair of human nature. Out of mutual distrust of their own humanity people are careful to interpose between each other for the purposes of commerce and intercourse something deliberately inhuman: the law. The great Livy, a man who had succeeded better than any other in the time of Augustus in preserving pure and intact the old Roman spirit—perhaps because he sat apart and made no noise—the great Livy says that "the law is deaf and inexorable, unrelenting and remorseless even toward venial offenses." [10] An admirable definition of the law, indeed. According to it, the law is as firm as rock, of the nature of stone rather than of human

[10] Liv. II, 3.

flesh. Before it, all men are equal. Whatever differences of rank, obligation, and class the law may establish, any and all derive from law itself. No man, however privileged by the law, is distinguished from any other in his relation to the precepts of law; whereas in a monarchy the subject lives under the law, but the monarch is merged with it, and a personal will may take the place of legal ordinances—a state of affairs which to a people with an extremely acute sense of law must seem entirely unendurable.

This negative sense of *libertas* as "life without kings" necessarily connotes a positive supplement which is "public life according to the traditional institutions of Republican Rome." This is the second and more concrete meaning that Cicero associates with the term. Thus Cicero felt free when he was ruled by magistracies, according to such laws as Rome's past had established up to his time. But these laws did not grant any of the liberties proclaimed by European liberalism, nor indeed any other liberties of that kind. *The political constitution of Rome was never "liberal."* And yet Cicero felt free under it; and when he saw it vanish he crouched in his villa at Tusculum like a badly wounded dog in his kennel, and there was no end of mournful howls for *libertas, libertas.*

Here we have reached the point where we can discern the difference between Roman *libertas* and that conception of freedom which has been the perennial principle of European political inspiration, nineteenth-century liberalism being only one of its expressions. In view of the fact that man can no more escape political rule than he can escape the weight of his body and the hunger of his stomach, he may adopt one of two fundamentally different attitudes, asking either "*Who* shall rule?" or, no matter who rules, "*How far* will I let myself be ruled?" The first question asks about the bearer of public power, the second about its limit.

European man, up to the present day, has been incessantly and keenly alive to the latter. He did not care so much who ruled—king, parliament, the people—but he wished to control the limits of this rule. These limitations or liberties have varied in various times. In feudalism they went under the names of privileges and immunities. European man never allowed public power to invade the entire realm of his personal life. The law itself was expected to delineate the private precinct where its sway ended.

Hence the word privi-lege which to a Roman would have sounded like a contradiction in terms. *Privilegium,* as a matter of fact, meant the opposite from what we understand by it; it meant "law against particular individuals." And in this sense it so horrified Cicero that he declared: "Our ancestors desired that no laws against particular individuals should be proposed; for that is what a privilege comes to. For nothing would be more unjust than such a law, when the very word law implies a decree or command that is binding upon all." [11]

In the Roman conception public power has no limits; it is total. A human being cannot be conceived of apart from the community to which he belongs. Man is man only as a member of a city. The city comes first. It is not a sum of individuals but a legally organized body with its own collective structure. The individual can exist and act politically only through public organs: *curia, tribus, centuria.* Directly and by himself, he can do nothing.

Such a conception of the individual and the state is in keeping with the general Roman conception of human life and the universe. A Roman regarded living not as a purely interhuman affair. Living meant living together with the gods who were, above all, gods of the community. An individual could not address the gods directly; Rome knew no "freedom of worship." The city had her magistrates, one of whom was in charge of communicating with the gods through long established rituals.

Nor could an individual harangue the people, a right connected with certain magistracies. Hence no "freedom of speech."

[11] *De legibus* III, 19.

For a private person to address himself directly to the populace was one of the most revolutionary and criminal acts a Roman could think of.

Cicero, it is true, laments the loss of *libera oratio*, and Tiberius treats himself to declaring in the senate, in the early part of his reign, that "in a free state speech and thought must be free." [12] But let us not make a mistake; what Cicero and Tiberius refer to is not the same as our freedom of speech; it is the freedom of speech of magistrates and senators, that is, an attribute of rule as such, not a liberty of individuals.

An analysis of the sturdy institution that was the Roman family would likewise disclose an absolute lack of private liberty. Indeed, such a precinct of privacy, guarded and secured against public interference, would have appeared to the Quirites as a sort of Indian reservation.

LIFE IN FREEDOM AND LIFE AS ADAPTATION

Between these two different styles of freedom, the Roman and the European, it would be absurd to decree arbitrarily that it is ours that is right. Let us rather recognize that people are free—in the political sense—when they live under institutions they prefer, no matter what those institutions are. In that case, our "liberal" constitutions would guarantee liberty not because they are "liberal" but because they are the form of government that most appeals to the political taste of the Western world. Our problem thus boils down to the question: What does it mean that people prefer such and such institutions?

It does not mean—as my reader, like myself, may at first think—that Cicero felt at ease under his time-honored institutions simply because they were old and he had got reconciled to them through habit and tradition. Cicero was a conservative but he was no traditionalist. He knew that the institutions he summarized under the title *libertas* had not been immutable figures in Roman history; that after slowly evolving as circum-

[12] *Suetonius* 28.

stances demanded, they had, once established, undergone constant change, emerging eventually with a physiognomy entirely different from the original. Furthermore, Cicero dedicated his own book *On the State*—written between 54 and 52, a time of relative and apparent political peace—to the purpose of preparing the ground for a grave constitutional reform, which he himself found it very hard to adopt, but which he hoped might guarantee survival of a torso of Republican institutions.

Generally speaking, mere permanence of institutions over a long stretch of time does not suffice to produce a feeling of ease and freedom. Proof of this, on an enormous scale, is given by the Roman Empire which lasted five centuries—as long as the Republic—without ever becoming truly familiar to the Romans themselves. Rome lived through her Empire in a chronic state of perplexity, never knowing today what this Empire, as a political institution, would look like tomorrow. Those who became accustomed to the Empire were the conquered peoples who came to believe in Rome's eternity—*Roma aeterna*—and allowed the reality, or rather the idea, of the Empire to linger on as late as the eighteenth century.

It is therefore permissible to say that the liking of a nation for certain institutions is an independent phenomenon which cannot be explained by habit. For further elucidation of this irreducible phenomenon, the following remarks may be made.

A state always and essentially exerts pressure upon the individuals who constitute it. Proceeding by means of domination and rule, it cannot help making itself felt as coercion. As man is born into, and exists in, a "physical world" composed of solid bodies which obstruct his freedom of motion, so he is born into, and inexorably exists in, a "social world" composed of anonymous pressures, which are exerted upon him in the form of uses, customs, valid norms, etc. The state is but one, if the strongest, among such social pressures. The limitation of our free will which the state unquestionably implies is of the same order as that imposed upon our muscles by the hardness of bodies, and therefore must be recognized as an inalienable part of the make-up of man. A society is not a man-made institution, as eighteenth-century philosophers thought, but a condition in which man finds himself irremediably and without any hope of true escape. Here we have come upon what I think must be regarded as the first principle of sociology. But for our present purpose it is unnecessary to dwell upon its importance.

The fact that state means pressure must be taken into account before we can begin to look for the distinguishing features between free and unfree public life. Political freedom cannot be defined as absence of pressure; for that situation does not exist. The decisive point lies in the fashion in which pressure is brought to bear. Are we not at any moment subject to the pressure of the atmosphere? Yet when this pressure affects us in a certain way, it imparts a glorious sense of "free movement." And the leather strap that, girding our loins, fosters a carriage of springy ease will, tied around our wrists, make us cry out to heaven that we are manacled.

The pressure of state becomes manifest in the form of "institutions." With this remark we have definitely cornered our problem. Man is not free to elude the permanent pressure of the collective body upon his person. But certain nations in certain epochs succeeded in giving that coercion institutional forms of which they fully approved; *they shaped the state after their vital preferences.* This is what we call "life in freedom."

But there are other times when, for multiple reasons, the *possibility* of preferring one institution to another vanishes even for those fortunate nations, and institutions impose themselves as by inexorable mechanical necessity. Nobody wants them; but there is no margin left for free option. Such a state of affairs has nothing to do with "tyranny." In comparison with the situation we are here trying to delineate, tyranny is a rather superficial phenomenon, a political anecdote springing up ephemerally in epochs of free life and presupposing a state of freedom, as can be observed in the Greek tyrannies before Alexander. In our case, it is not only that the pressure of state as such assumes a character of duress, but that the concrete institutions, in so far as they are effective and no mere slogan, descend upon the social body to the frank disgust of everyone, including those who seemingly enforce them, yet, in truth, are themselves merely the visible organs of an invisible historical mechanism.

In such times human life does not flow freely and easily through institutional channels built *with its approval* and made to measure for it. There is no eager and at bottom always cheerful effort on the part of life to accommodate the rigidity of the state to its own tastes, as expressed in the form of so-called ideals or so-called conventions. Life is converted into the opposite of all this, into spiritless *adaptation of each individual existence to the iron mold of the state*. This is what we call "life as adaptation."

It is not that in epochs such as these people like to adapt themselves, that such is their preference, but that public life ceases to be a question of liking; that there is no choice. In a strange automatic way the state assumes an attitude of unmitigated exaction toward the individual, accepting no conditions, no reservations, no objections, not even collaboration, nothing short of pure and simple surrender. Collaboration is possible only in secondary fields, not in the most exalted function of state, in ruling. Adaptation being the integral form of life, there is no way of escaping it. After Caesar has triumphed, Cato may commit suicide in Utica; but with his suicide he performs only the most desperate form of adaptation.

In the foregoing we have advanced a theorem. Theorems are imaginary figures with contours of geometrical neatness. But reality never exactly coincides with theorems. And yet there is no other manner of understanding reality than to fit, as best we can, its perpetually shifting shapes into such prefabricated molds as our imagination produces. Theorems allow us to take our bearings in the chaos of reality. They may even supply the means to determine the discrepancy between reality and the cobweb of our ideas. Thinking is an ironical operation. It enables us to ascertain the "pure truth." But it also reveals that facts never quite conform; for facts are the impure truth.

Were we now to examine by the light of our theorem the entire political history of Rome with all the wealth of its contradictions and meanderings, the reader, I hope, would not find our theorem guilty of undue exaggeration. But I must confine myself to indicating with a few swift strokes the general outline of the historical process that ended in the Empire.

The expulsion of the kings is the opening scene of Rome's life in liberty. It bears all the features characteristic of this form of political existence. Cicero, in accordance with legend, holds the abuses and usurpations of the kings responsible for the Republican revolution. Revolutions are prone to be explained this way; it is the explanation of politicians, not of historians, an explanation handy for meetings and editorials. Yet it would seem characteristic of revolution, in contrast with revolt, that a revolution abolishes uses, not abuses. Old uses in which people had lived at ease begin one day to seem unbearable. That is what happened in Rome.

The kings represented the predominance of the Etruscan element. Under their sway, the civilization of Latium progressed. Rome was built, her name being Etruscan. The population increased and prospered. The Greek cities on Sicily, in Campania, and on the heel and toe of Italy sent from afar vague waves of cultural inspiration: minute images of gods; rites; tales of martial adventure; political dreams. A new life, yet crude but brimming with sturdy appetites and inspiring projects, burst forth from the archaic Latin roots with all the vigor of spring.

Is it felt as a public exigency to eliminate the kings? How urgent was it to put an end to monarchism? Obviously not to the degree of an inevitable necessity. On the contrary: that abolishment of monarchic government should be felt as a necessity already represented a creative act, a fervid urge spontaneously sprung up in the minds. Thus the grudge against kings was not primary, not the cause, but secondary, the effect of something that had previously stirred in the souls. The impulse to revolution came from a new and fascinating vision of state organization. The state was to be ruled not by a personal will but by an anonymous imperative in the shaping of which all citizens were, more or less, to collaborate and which was to speak through the organ of the law. The ruler thus would cease to rule on his own account and after his own taste. Renouncing his personality, he would become an automaton dispensing law. "It can truly be said that the magistrate is a speaking law, and the law a silent magistrate." [13] This idea spontaneously springing from the innermost Roman imagination—as spring from imagination poetic images to which this idea is, after all, akin—grew into an "ideal" and began to exert its irresistible suction on the will. For ideals exert suction on the mind. The simple presence of such an idea was sufficient to let the existence of kings seem unendurable.

Here we have an illustration of the way in which any change —revolutionary or evolutionary—is brought about in epochs of political freedom. All events come to pass in liberty—that is, spontaneously springing from deep-rooted inspiration. Hence the strange reversal of the seemingly natural chronological order between the solution and the need it meets. For it so happens that the solution, the ideal, comes first, and that it creates, if not the need itself, awareness of it. In other words, such a need is not absolute and inevitable. That is precisely why people are *pleased* to pretend that it is a necessity; and only because of this does it then become a necessity. Danton expressed this *priority of the ideal* when he said in the Convention (August 13, 1793): "The revolution lived in people's souls at least twenty years before it came to be proclaimed."

In periods of life as adaptation, things look entirely different. In such times political exigencies present themselves with an

[13] *De legibus* III, 1.

absolute and inescapable character; and they do, not because
we think of them so—what with all their frightfulness one
would as lief disregard them altogether—but precisely because
they allow of no true solution. For let us be clear about this:
what people are ready to call wholeheartedly a solution is sure
to be nothing if not the "ideal" one. Anything short of this is
called, and strictly speaking is, no solution but a remedy, a mere
device that is accepted because it cannot be helped. The Roman
Empire provides the most gigantic instance, in time and space,
of an irremediable remedy.

We thus may state that public life assumes the luminous
aspect of freedom if the following conditions are fulfilled:
(1) that the collectivity is not confronted with pressing internal problems, anarchy for instance; (2) that in political changes
the solution, at least in its general outline, precedes the problems and is instrumental in bringing them about, or in other
words, that the collective mind is actuated by genuine "ideals
of public life"; (3) that every member of the society feels that
he participates in one way or another in the function of ruling
and thus plays an active part in the state.

These three conditions were fulfilled in the history of Rome
from the expulsion of the kings until 50 B.C. The precision of the
date has, of course, merely symbolic significance; however, 50
B.C. is the year in which Cicero's laments at the loss of liberty
began. Can this decisive and irrevocable change in Roman public life be regarded as a mere contingency which might have been
avoided, or are we to believe that there will, for every "free"
society, come a moment in its history when mechanical adaptation is the sole form of life left to it? Moreover, supposing experience shows that the latter invariably happened in the past,
does that mean that any future society will suffer the same fate?
Bodily diseases were thought incurable until new treatments
brought them under control. Is some kind of medicine of collective life, a therapeutics of society, completely out of the
question? This much is clear: if anything of the sort is possible
it will be a matter of research, not of politics.

HISTORY IN THE ASCENDANT

The political history of Rome, her growth and elastic expansion from the crude village of the seven hills to the marble city that the emperors built, has an ascending rhythm of such perfection as is peculiar not to history but to music only. This consummation lends to Roman history the dignity of a paradigm and makes it "classical" in the fullest sense of the word. Greece, said Mommsen, is the prototype of human progress, Rome of national. The first may be questioned—human endeavor transcends art and science—the second not. Compared with the history of Rome, the political histories of Asia and Africa—even that of Greece, though for different reasons—have a certain infrahuman, plantlike aspect; they are suffered rather than inspired. Those nations did not *make* their own history in epic fight against fate and chance. But Rome's political destiny down to Julius Caesar springs from the Romans as the jet from the fountain.

After the expulsion of the kings, the Republic preserved the simple structure of the monarchic state: a council of elders made up of the chiefs of the old families (*gentes*) and a magistrate appointed by election, who was in charge of the executive function, command of the army, and enforcement of the law; his original name is likely to have been *praetor*. So plain a form of state sufficed for a germinant nation. But as the collective body grew more numerous and more diversified, social groups or classes developed. Generation after generation, the old families had gone on accumulating the triple treasure that permits establishment of an aristocracy: nobility, wealth, proficiency. A "nobleman," we remember, is a man who is "known" (*notus*) —that is, known before he has done anything himself, not for his own merit but for the deeds of his forebears which are present in every man's mind as soon as his family name is mentioned. In the same way wealth and proficiency are accumulated by inheritance—particularly in early times—and belong to families rather than to individuals. The three together secure to their

owners social preponderance over what we may call the Unknown Citizen and what in Rome was the *plebs*—a word of
doubtful origin but somehow conveying a notion of multitude.
The plebeian population soon increased considerably, and it
was their growing number from which they first derived their
social power. That is why in Greece these two groups were
called "the few" and "the many"—most felicitous names which
should never be abandoned.

It is admirable how the Roman Republic, step by step, fits
the growing complexity of society with new institutions, splitting up the supreme power and delegating it to a multiplicity
of interlinked powers or *potestates*. The praetor cedes the supreme power over the city and the army to two new magistrates: the *consules* whose conjoint or twin action precludes the
tyranny of one man. The *praetores* continue being entrusted
with the execution of private law. The *ediles* take care of the
city. The *quaestores* are in charge of the management of the
revenue.

Any important change in the social structure of a community
entails a public exigency which, if it is authentic, raises a question of state. For the state is the social agency that is concerned
with the management of what is necessary, indispensable. It is
exciting indeed to watch how to each of such changes the political inventive power of the Romans answers with a new institution as precise, concrete, ingenious, and original as the
work of a master engineer. Any one of these institutions, which
are neither abstract humbug nor an expression of vague re-
formatory urges, comes so unfailingly at the right moment,
starts functioning with such ease, and fits so naturally into
the existing politico-juridical organism that it is like the chim-
ing in of the flute or the horn in the singing pattern of a symphony.

Or in another metaphor: the state envelops the social body
as smoothly and elastically as the skin covers the living body.
The skin also presses tightly to the body, but it adjusts itself to
every bend and swelling of the muscles so that we feel perfectly

free in it. Indeed, there is no better expression for the feeling of freedom than to say that we are as much at ease as in our own skin. Let us note the paradox herein contained; a pressure exercised against me is felt as mine, as forming a part of myself. What in our abstract theorem we have named "life in liberty" may now more graphically be called "the state as skin." In epochs of "life as adaptation" the state is not felt as a skin but as an orthopedic apparatus.

An institution that is the conclusive answer to a political problem is utterly unlikely to emerge from a situation in which there is no choice and measures have to be adopted mechanically for want of any alternatives. Political imagination must have been free to consider various solutions and to select among them the one that best fits the circumstances as well as the general idea of life operative in the collective mind.

So little imposed by necessity were those institutions with which the Romans met their public conflicts that to us, when we see them emerge in the history of that nation, they always come as a surprise, expedient and unforeseeable, the discovery of genius. They are not inspirations derived from abstract reasonings—like all those patterns of constitutions which European philosophers since the seventeenth century have never tired of concocting, and which make such tiresome reading—but inspirations evolved by circumstance from the depths of unswerving beliefs such as constitute the soul of a nation while a nation possesses a soul.

THE TRIBUNATE OF THE PEOPLE OR A SUBLIME IRRATIONALITY

A good illustration of the foregoing is furnished by the tribunate of the people. Let us try to visualize the situation. The commonalty, through their steadily increasing number and their share in the wars of the city, had become a social factor of some moment. The new distribution of social weight called for redistribution of public power. The state had to be adapted to the new muscle of the social body that was the common peo-

ple. Or, without euphemistic allegories, the people had to be
given their share in government.

But the plebeians were—and were to remain for a long time
—the healthy populace of a society in its prime, not the insolent,
unruly masses of later historical stages. They believed with living faith in the same picture of the universe and of life in which
the patricians believed. They believed in Rome and her destiny
with which they felt united for better and for worse. They believed in the proficiency of the ruling class who had fought their
battles year after year and won wealth, land, and glory for the
commonwealth. Nonetheless, and not less resolutely for that—
with the Romans of the great times all is vigor and purpose—
they wanted to participate in government. Yet as they knew
that they were ignorant of state affairs—diplomacy, strategy,
law, administration—it was clear to them that their part in government could not be of a directing, positive character. The
patricians, on the other hand, a hard and fearless lot who were
engrossed in making their own Rome, had no mind to let the
Republic be governed by whoever happened to come along.

Hence long and obstinate struggles; struggles, no revolution.
For underground, the contestants were welded together by
profound concord based on common beliefs and on an imperturbable common aspiration to grow into one people. That is
the reason why the plebeians chose, as their supreme weapon,
that mildest possible device the noble tale of which used to
move us so deeply in the days of our childhood. They left
the city as a body with their leaders at their head and occupied first the Sacred Mount and then the Aventine Hill. In those
times cities grew on hills. To occupy a hill was the symbol for
founding a new city in face of the old. Revolutionary masses
who fight not for definite, concrete reforms but for the over-
throw of the state and a new magical structure to rise on its
ruins would have done the opposite. Instead of threatening to
found a new city, they would have seized the old and killed or
expelled the aristocrats. The hour was to come when Roman
commoners would enter the bloody, disgusting zone of revolu-

tion. For the time being they were content to threaten secession. The patricians gave in.

And what was the outcome? Fichte said, with reference to Napoleon, that the secret of great policy simply consists in "actualizing that which is." The leader of the multitude entered the government under the name of the tribune of the people; that is, he became a magistrate with the character of representative of the plebeians—not of the city as such.

From the standpoint of pure reason, to entrust *part* of the community, or a party as such, with ruling power over the *whole* community must appear unwise and irrational. Moreover, this magistrate, who was no magistrate proper and did not enjoy the honors connected with office, ruled in a highly efficient way and yet without ruling, properly speaking. The tribune could not submit a bill; he could only prevent—and fulminantly prevent—that a bill be passed. His main contribution to government was the veto. Like the basilisk, which paralyzed whatever living being came before its eyes, the tribune could with one gesture suspend action of any other magistrate including the consuls. He could freeze the entire state machinery. Thus his ruling power consisted in preventing abuse of power; what he exercised was a curb on power, a counterpower.

For that purpose he was endowed with a privilege, more effective than all honors: his person was sacred, inviolable, taboo. Whoever touched a tribune was a dead man.

The institution of the tribunate, which rationalistic theories of state law esteem an absurdity, was the prodigious implement of state that insured for centuries the solidarity beween the senate and the people, between patricians and plebeians. Assuming the year 471 B.C. to be the approximate date of its establishment, we may observe that for three centuries and a half the tribunate kept Rome from sliding down the *montagne Russe* of revolution. And who knows whether Roman concord might not have lasted much longer, had Rome continued to live enclosed in herself and true to her own spirit. But her unequaled triumph over the world around her laid her open, *intellectually unde-*

fended, to foreign influences of perilous potency. We must not forget that Tiberius Gracchus, the first Roman revolutionary, kept in his household a Graeculus called Blossius, a rationalistic philosopher of barren ways, an intellectual spider, spinning the web of unprofitable utopias.

The strong Rome of the creative centuries was Rome of the S.P.Q.R.—*Senatus Populusque Romanus*. That robust caste of men who had not enough imagination to be hypocrites, and who took reality at its face value, ever recognized the fact that every city is made up of two quasi cities and that national unity is the unity of at least two elements: the rich and the poor, the illustrious and the nameless, the creative (or *poietikos*) and the vulgar, *senatus populusque*—each of which is endowed with its own rights. I will resist the temptation of analyzing these two names, particularly *populus*, a word bodeful and pregnant like the cloud wherein the thunder travels. Let me merely state that the primitive meaning of *populari* was "to lay waste," "to depopulate." But be that as it may, the duality of senate and people hinged upon the tribunate through which the plebeians exerted their growing influence on government, as more and more able men arose from their ranks.

Moreover, when five centuries later the Roman Republic had vanished and nothing remained of all its time-honored magistracies but the ignominy into which they had fallen, when a dozen ferocious civil wars had wiped out all vestiges of liberty, and the heavy flood of murder had left *forum* and *curia* covered with clots of purple blood, and the universal anguish sent the survivors looking for a man who might, with absolute power, rebuild some sort of state and revive government—there was but one political institution left that could give legal support to that man's seizure of power: the tribunate of the people. Of the venerable galley Rome, run upon the rocks in total shipwreck, the figurehead alone, that "absurd" institution of the tribunate, was left floating above the waves. "Augustus," we read in Tacitus,[14] "revived the name of the highest office [the

[14] *Annales* III, 56.

tribunitian power] so that he need not assume the name of king
or dictator and yet might bear a title that left no doubt as to his
pre-eminence over all other powers."

THEORY OF COMPLEMENTS IN COLLECTIVE LIFE

We have thought it necessary, instead of dealing simply in
the abstract with what we called inspired or preferred institutions, to give an account of the general character of at least one
such institution. But the office of the dictator would have answered our purpose as well. It is another example of that Roman
realism which made no bones about admitting that in societies
normalcy is only too abnormal. Everyday affairs were appropri-
ately taken care of by the powers of the consuls and the prae-
tors; but it was also incumbent upon the law to provide without
squeamishness as to means for emergencies arising from external threat or internal frenzy. To such emergencies the dictator-
ship was the answer. However, Roman legal symbolism required that the dictator be elected in the darkness of night.

I have preferred the tribunate for our main example because the character of this institution accentuates the problem
to which I wish to dedicate this last section.

What we have said regarding the tribunate may be summarized as follows: (1) The tribunate bestows executive—and not
only advisory—power upon a magistrate who represents the interests and aspirations of only part of the community. Moreover,
the tribune is endowed with the right of veto, an extremely easy
and convenient vehicle of political action. In view of this, abstract reasoning inevitably comes to the conclusion that such an
institution is impossible because it cannot fail to lead to a
chronic deadlock of the governmental machine and thus to
pave the way for *coups d'états* or revolutions in order to remove
the obstacle. (2) The fact is that this institution enjoyed a long
and glorious existence.

Why, then, is it that our "pure reason" should be thus mistaken? Very simply because it treats as an isolate—abs-tract—

object a thing that never does or can occur isolated. An institution as it functions *in reality* is not circumscribed by the form
laid down for it in the law. It functions interlocked with others.
Moreover—and here things begin to look interesting—the ag-
gregate of all of them, the state, works in indissoluble concert
with all other social activities that are distinct from the state—
distinct but inseparable. Collective life is a system of functions
which presuppose, limit, and support one another. The reality of
an institution cannot be reduced to its legal form proper. Origins and ends of an institution lie in other social forces by which
it is maintained and regulated.

Evidence of this is to be found in the institution of the tribunate. The tribune was the representative in government of the
interests of the commoners. But these commoners were not any
abstract masses. They were Roman plebeians to whom for many
centuries the destiny of Rome mattered as much as their own
interests; whose firm religious and secular beliefs set up within
each individual the curbs of discipline and obedience; and who
looked with spontaneous respect upon the nobility, proficiency,
and wealth of their aristocracy. This is a fact—duplicated, by
the way, in England only a generation ago—that cannot be discovered by pure thinking but must be narrated by history. Once
this fact is known, the tribunate, which to rationalistic theories
appears absurd and incomprehensible, turns out to be a most
natural and intelligible thing. What remains opaque to "pure
reason" becomes lucid to narrative or "historical reason."

The tribunate of the people was the legal instrument through
which the commonalty brought to bear upon government their
disagreements with the senate. Such a thing could be done without grave upheavals because the people's dissent did not ex-
clude their wholehearted loyalty to the senate itself and the
entire life of Rome. Thus the institution worked owing to something apart from it and from the state; it worked by virtue of a
complement obtaining somewhere in the ultralegal depths of
society. Once more we find the law leaning upon customs. Hor-
ace's sentence *leges sine moribus vanae*—"laws without customs

are vain"—may be regarded as one of the main principles of sociology, provided the vague form of the wording is interpreted by means of a theory of the extralegal complements required by each law.

Here we begin to understand that each authentic institution is untransferable. Supposing we wanted to lift it out of its native soil, where should we cut it? Where begin and where end those political entities which language, owing to its magical power of creating phantoms, puts before us as independent and self-sustaining objects, calling them by the definite names of "tribunate of the people," "parliament," "freedom of the press"? None of these institutions terminates in a clear-cut line. They all reach back into the particular collective life where they originated and whence they receive their indispensable supplements, their strength and their control. He who wishes to transplant an institution from one people to another must bring along with it that people in its verity and reality.

Laws of foreign nations may serve as incitement and even as guidance—Rome not infrequently took her bearings from the juridical conceptions of Greece—but in the last instance every nation must invent for itself. Imitation of alien political institutions betrays a pathological state of society. A people cannot take its institutions from the manifest surface of foreign nations; it must discover them in its own innermost being if it wants to lead a life in freedom. Freedom cannot be achieved by proclaiming a few random liberties. Life in liberty presupposes a perfect continuity of circulation throughout the collective body, from the heart of its common beliefs to the skin which is the state, and back from the skin to the bowels of faith.

Notes on Thinking —
Its Creation of the World
AND
Its Creation of God

Contents

CRISIS OF THE INTELLECTUAL AND
CRISIS OF THE INTELLECT

IT IS time we gave some thought to thinking. For of all things thinking is perhaps the one that has of late gone most definitely out of fashion. Going out of fashion is fatal to what has never been more than a fashion. But when something substantive, essential, and perennial finds itself outmoded, it need not be depressed. It then realizes that in its time of splendor, riding the crest of the wave, it lived alienated from its sole self. And only as it enjoys a respite from general attention has it returned into its own and again become itself in as pure nay in a purer manner than during that other unique hour, the hour of its beginning, when it grew in secret, untalked of by other people, free from alien temptation, and capable of singleness of purpose.

These reflections do not occur to me on the spur of the moment. They may be found trotting along on many a bypath throughout my work. I have been expecting the present situation of thinking, and I have foretold it. In an earlier essay, "Reform of the Intellect," [1] I gave my apprehensions the following expression:

A situation like this requires that the intellectuals should withdraw from the social heights and concentrate upon their own concerns. This withdrawal will have to be effected slowly, step by step. The affairs intellectuals have become involved in are too many to be abandoned without warning. But as to the general course there can be no mistake. The intellectual minority must be expected to divest their work of all political or humanitarian "pathos," and to renounce being

---

[1] The essay, first published in *La Nación*, Buenos Aires, 1923, was later included in the volume *Goethe desde dentro* (Goethe from Within), Revista de Occidente, 1933. In it I advanced my reasons why I thought advisable what elsewhere I had called the withdrawal of the intellectual into the background, and if need be into the catacombs of the social scene.

taken seriously by the multitude. In other words, research must cease
to be considered a public affair and must become a private concern
of such individuals as feel spontaneously driven to it.

And what a relief to the intellect to be rid of the cumbersome tasks
it rashly took on! How delightful to go freely about its own subtle
pursuits, again to be bent upon itself, to live at the fringe of the busy
world unharassed by the necessity of producing premature solutions,
and to let the problems unfold according to their inherent powers of
expansion.

Such a withdrawal by parsimonious steps, without desertion,
from the service of life as "collective life" leaves the thinker severed
from his fellow men, in unmitigated solitude. When this has come
to pass and he is thrown upon himself, thinking assumes a new aspect. The attention of other people tempts the scholar to think for
them. But since they exist in the plural, in the form of a collective
body, and as such have no other life than that deriving from their
external interests, research done in their service becomes utilitarian
in the bad sense of the word. In contrast to such "servility" of the intellect to spurious life, the Greeks already recognized the genuine
exercise of the intellectual faculty as being of the "nonutilitarian"
character of pure contemplation.

But when a man is thus left to himself he discovers that his intellect begins to work for him and in the service of his solitary life, a
life without external interests but laden with personal risks and intimate concerns. It will then dawn upon him that pure contemplation
or disinterested use of the intellect is an illusion and that "pure
thinking" is a practice and a technique also; a technique of and for
genuine life, what Juan de la Cruz called the "sonorous solitude" of
life. And with this insight the radical reform of the intellect begins.

When the foregoing was written intellectuals still enjoyed
great social prestige, in certain respects the greatest they have
ever possessed in the course of history. It is unnecessary to
dwell upon the change of condition they have, with few excep-
tions, experienced since. As a consequence research work has
been brought low, so low, indeed, that during recent years the
number of those who have really had a contribution to make has
been quite incredibly small. For a curious pre-established har-

mony seems to prevail, according to which epochs in which freedom of thinking suffers radical political curtailment would tend to coincide with epochs in which intellectuals have nothing or little to say about human matters. This may account for the disconcerting phenomenon of the *saecula obscura,* the murky centuries, which unexpectedly open before the eyes of the historian like abysses of darkness. If those ages seem all but mute, it is not only because public upheavals left no respite for tranquil writing but also because scholars lacked clear and vivid ideas to be committed to writing. As an example take the tenth century in Europe. A curious oscillation is noticeable in the five centuries of the Roman Empire. Phases of relative— never abundant—clarity alternate with others of dense fog.

It is a fact that thinking is out of fashion. In a few years the place in society occupied by the "life intellectual" has changed completely. This by itself would be enough to give thinking the cue to reflect on its own fate. But it is another motive that has inspired the following notes—for that is what they are, hence their somber dryness. The social situation of the intellectual is an extrinsic and a surface problem, in comparison with the intellectual situation of the intellect itself.

It is within thinking, in its inmost recesses, that a peripety is happening for which we are at a loss to find an equal in European history. A perfunctory survey may disclose some similarity to the crisis of ideas that began in the fifteenth century. But the parallel is no sooner drawn than it turns out to be inadequate for quantity as well as quality. The present crisis is more sweeping and reaches deeper. Besides, its character is in a certain way inverse to that of the great spiritual drama we are wont to call the Renaissance. At that time thinking felt that it must progress from little to ever more. It passed through a crisis of puberty with all the moral peculiarities of such a crisis. Suffice it to quote Lorenzo Valla's rhapsodic outburst: "I have taught men two thousand new things!" The present crisis cannot simply be described as the opposite of this, a shrinking. Only a crude diagnosis would attribute it offhand to a sense of deficiency. Rather it looks as though thinking had become conscious of its own plenitude. For plenitude abides not with youth as is often foolishly believed but with maturity. Youth, as it is given to excess, lives in an illusion of boundless possibilities, while maturity, precisely because it has reached its fullness, and that is its limits, has also discovered its limitation. Maturity is the pull at the reins that curbs the irresponsible ravings of youth. It doubtless means a certain contraction and resignation. But not from want; on the contrary, maturity has come to such plenitude that it can devolve part of itself in order to restrain and regulate the rest.

The concrete meaning and the validity of these observations will appear only after we have gone the whole length of our subject. Here we need only state that the present inner crisis of thinking is such that we refrain from likening it offhand to any other that has occurred in Europe's past. And this statement should not be taken as advancing any diagnosis. We know that something important is happening to human thinking, but we do not know what it is, and we know even less whether it is good or bad.

In the present crisis of thinking two different strands are discernible. The more palpable and visible one consists in the so-called crisis of the foundations which has arisen in the three exemplary sciences: mathematics, physics, and logic. These three sciences have, for the last three centuries, been esteemed the purest and strongest representatives of thinking. From their substantial solidity derived the faith in reason on which the most cultured of men have lived throughout this epoch. Any slight vacillation in these prototypes of science cannot but cause a sense of insecurity in the entire sphere of intellectual activity. As it is, their extraordinary advance has, for these thirty years, been accompanied by a growing restlessness. Physicists, mathematicians, and logicians have, for the first time in the history of their sciences, come upon problems concerning the fundamental principles of their theoretical constructions. It is precisely in the foundations—the basis on which their intellectual operations repose—and not in such or such special parts of the theoretical edifice that disquieting signs have appeared.

Yet beneath this stratum of the present crisis there lies another more fundamental one. Apart from, and independent of, what has been happening in exact sciences, a crisis has arisen in the general attitude of men toward thinking as such. As a first description of this tremendous fact, I quote the following passage from Husserl:

The present situation of European sciences calls for fundamental reflection. These sciences have lost the Great Faith in themselves, in their absolute meaning. Modern man of our day, in contrast with "modern man" of the Enlightenment, does not conceive science and the new civilization shaped by it as the self-objectivation of human reason, or as the universal function created by mankind in order to attain for itself a truly satisfactory life, an individual and social life directed by practical reason. This Great Faith, which at a certain time took the place of religious faith and which believes that science leads to wisdom—to an actually rational knowledge of man, the world, and God and through this to a life ever capable of improvement, but verily and from the outset worth living, a life in happiness, contentment, and well-being—this faith has doubtless lost its power in wide circles. That is why we now live in a world that has become incomprehensible to us, a world in which people strive in vain to find the purpose and the meaning of their doing that were once so clearly known and fully acknowledged by intellect and will.[2]

No one at all conversant with the significance of Husserl— the most influential figure in philosophy for nearly a century— can help reading these lines without deep emotion: first because of the catastrophe they foretell; second because Husserl as a thinker is an extreme rationalist—in fact the last great rationalist, who proposed to adopt as his own the starting point of the first, the great Descartes, so that Husserl's philosophy represents the quintessence of rationalism; third because whoever knows Husserl knows that what he said he had "seen"; fourth because this represents, I believe, the one and only place in all

[2] Edmund Husserl, *Formale und transzcendentale Logik*, Max Niemeyer Halle, 1929, pp. 4, 5.

his work where he makes mention of a fact that transcends and encompasses science proper—that is, a universal human fact; fifth and last because Husserl lived aloof and never roamed about to gather "information." How pressing must have been that fact which he described so soberly if it penetrated into his seclusion and obtruded itself on him so that he could not help "seeing" it!

However, I must add two observations. First, in my opinion the "fundamental reflection" that forms the subject matter of Husserl's above-quoted work appears to me by no means fundamental, as I shall presently show.[3] The second observation refers to Husserl's description as such. Husserl, as I have said, never returned to this subject. He was only interested in stating it as briefly as possible. And on this understanding his exposition is sufficient and moving. But as this subject forms one of the main issues of the investigation in hand, we must at the threshold of our study be clear about Husserl's indications, lest a slight swerving from the right track at this stage degenerate later into the reader's becoming frankly lost.

Husserl observes that the sciences have lost the "Great Faith" in themselves, and he immediately repeats this, adding that present-day man has lost the "Great Faith" in reason which man of the Enlightenment possessed. Twice in a few lines he speaks of the "Great Faith." The vaguely quantitative term also is unique in Husserl's always extremely precise terminology. What does he mean by "Great Faith"? Is there a "Little Faith"? And what would be the difference between two objects that cannot be measured in inches and yards? The vagueness, we hardly need say so, is deliberate. Anybody who can read will have noticed that the most exact author occasionally prefers an expression of wider margin in which the idea, like the clapper in the bell, may move at ease. His motives are clear. Unable for whatever reasons to develop his idea so as to make it intelligible in its strict form but loath, on the other hand, to betray its exact meaning, the writer chooses a phrase of blurred outline which

[3] Cf. p. 81.

some day may be replaced without inconsistency by a sharp contour. Of this Husserl's "Great Faith"—an expression so alien to his intellectual style—furnishes a good example.

Does Husserl mean to say that present-day man has completely lost faith in reason and that the sciences do entirely distrust themselves? Obviously not. Our world, he says, has grown "problematic" *because* the "Great Faith" has been lost. If what is lost were not only the "Great Faith" but the "Little Faith," too—absolutely all faith—the world would not be problematic, at least not on account of this loss. For a thing to be problematic it is necessary that we be not altogether convinced of its opposite being true. The "rational world" would not be problematic to us if we were persuaded that reason cannot be put to any use of importance and that we might as well write it off. In that case we should firmly believe in the radical irrationality of the world—a belief like any other and one, in fact, that has been held by other epochs.

But our situation is different. It is not that man has lost his faith in reason.[4] What has happened is this: In the seventeenth century the leading minorities of Europe began to feel radical confidence in the power of the intellect as the unique and universal instrument for solving the problems of living. This confidence permeated wider and wider social circles in the course of the eighteenth century and established itself in the nine-

---

[4] A discerning mind will hardly hold the real situation to be faithfully reflected in those disparaging statements abounding in contemporary literature in which reason or intellect is pronounced dead and buried. Such utterances refute themselves. Their own tenor and the contexts in which they occur reveal that the author's notion of reason or intellect is none too clear. I remember how amused I was when, as a mere boy, I came upon sentences like this in Tolstoi: "I who have studied all philosophical systems am convinced that they all are null and void." Tolstoi's books, fine though they are for other reasons, betray that the great man was far from having penetrated into any one philosophy.

However, the great positive movements of practical not theoretical orientation which are now arising in the world with the purpose of organizing human life according to declared irrational principles deserve full attention. Not that they show any sign of being clearly conscious of the case pending between man and his reason; but through their character as positive attempts at reform they are gathering useful experience which will eventually end in rediscovering reason—a reason cured of its vagaries.

teenth as a valid belief of the European communities. Faith in
reason knew no limits either regarding its own character of faith
or in what it expected of the intellect. Under these circumstances, man set himself to grounding his life on ideas as such.
Hence the fabulous production of scientific work: theories, doctrines—in short, ideas. But one day it became apparent that
intellect and reason, while producing more and more perfect
solutions for innumerable problems predominantly of material
order, failed in all their attempts to solve the others, the problems of mainly moral and social character, among them such as
were felt to raise ultimate and crucial questions. A sense of failure like this can arise only out of a great many abortive trials
that have been undertaken in the fullness of faith. Diffidence is
always a late chapter in the history of a confidence. As a result,
man finds himself in a state of suspense. On the one hand he
cannot help continuing to believe in the efficacity of his intellect
which goes on indefatigably solving new formidable problems.
Reason, he knows, is by no means a phantom doomed to vanish,
an illusion that can and must be exploded, but a very compact
reality which he can and must reckon with. On the other hand
to trust it with an unconditional and unlimited blank check is
no longer possible. But since reason was explicitly and precisely "that in which he could believe unconditionally," the object of his faith, and with it, as by rebound, the intrinsic character of that faith, have changed before his very eyes.

On the threshold of this study and by way of a first approximation, I think we may now describe our present inner situation with regard to reason and the intellect as follows: Lost in
the profusion of ideas produced by himself, man feels uncertain
what to do with them. He continues to believe that ideas serve
some true need, but he does not quite know which. All he knows
is that the service they may give is not what the last three centuries held it to be. *There is a strong feeling that reason will
have to occupy a new position in the system of activities that
constitute human life*. In short, from being the great solution the
intellect has grown to be the great problem. That is why it be-

hooves us to reflect on it, tackling the subject at its broadest and not confining it to one or another particular form of intellectual endeavor such as science or philosophy. These stand out as minute figures, belonging to a few centuries and a few regions of the planet, against the vast background of human intellectual occupation during a million years—the approximate age ascribed to our species by recent theories on glacial epochs. In this most comprehensive sense we ask ourselves: What is thinking? But before venturing on an answer we must clear the ground through a series of painful divorces between couples of ideas which tradition has persistently united.

THE MASKS OF THINKING

When we look for the phenomenon of thinking—thinking in its authentic form—where we have good reasons to expect it, we find ourselves beset by a swarm of things that pretend to be thinking but are not.

Nor is this plight peculiar to this special case. We look for the being, the true essence of a thing, and what first comes to hand is unfailingly and of necessity its trappings and its masks. Reality, as Heraclitus already observed, likes to hide.[5] The world is a constant carnival. Masks surround us. Forests cannot be seen for trees, trees for leaves, and so on. Being, the thing itself, remains essentially covered and hidden, *l'homme au masque de fer*. The operation through which we hope to espy it beneath its cloak is called ascertaining (making certain) or verifying (truth finding). To make patent what is hidden, we must discover, un-veil, de-nude it. And when the thing lies naked before us we say that we behold the truth—the "naked truth" being therefore tautological.[6]

The mechanism of such concealment is simple enough. The

[5] Fragment 123. φύσις κρύπτεσθαι φιλεῖ.
[6] For being as something essentially concealed and truth as discovery, cf. the author's book *Meditación del Quijote*, Madrid, 1914; or *Obras*, vol. I, pp. 20–26.

being of the thing, or, which is the same, the "thing itself" in its selfhood, is wrapped in all those phenomena that *"have to do with it"* but are not it. And our mind, on its journey toward the thing itself, begins by mistaking for the thing all that which "has to do with it"—thus enacting the eternal scene of the exit at dawn from the ball with the pretty mask. "What has to do with a thing" has to do with it more or less and sometimes very much indeed. The more, the worse; for the more stubborn will be the concealment and the longer will we remain confused and deceived.

Thus thinking hides behind a massive screen of psychological concepts referring to intellectual activities. The question "What is thinking?" is apt to be answered with a description of the psychic mechanisms that function when a man is thinking. These functions—to perceive, compare, abstract, judge, generalize, infer—obviously have to do with thinking. Without them, man would be incapable of performing the occupation called thinking. Thinking is a doing, something man *does* or decides to do —hence I call it an occupation—and not something that goes on within him like seeing, remembering, imagining, reasoning. It is characteristic of any "doing" that it is done *by* something *for* something, the third constituent being that *with* which it is done, the means or tool.[7] The means may be inadequate, in which case our doing falls short of its intended end; it is a frustrated doing, though not, for that reason, any less a doing.

Not only modern psychology but even Aristotle, as we shall soon see, identifies thinking with the simple execution of intellectual psychic activities, thereby committing a twofold error. For man in resolving to think does not simply set himself to perceiving, remembering, abstracting, inferring—all of which are pure intellectual mechanisms—but mobilizes these activities *for* a certain end. In fact, this end he is bent upon—and which we expect to explain later with more detail—furnishes a more concise definition of thinking than the instruments with which he

[7] The structural scheme of any doing or action may therefore be given as: something done *by, for,* and *with* something.

strives to reach it.[8] The second of the two errors consists in assuming that the means on which man relies for the task of thinking are adequate and sufficient to guarantee success. An ever-repeated, painful experience testifies to exactly the opposite. *The ends in pursuit of which man embarks upon thinking have never been satisfactorily attained; there is no getting around the fact that in this respect man's gifts have never come up to his intentions.* Thinking, we begin to discern from this preliminary level of our investigation, is an occupation to which man must dedicate himself, although he despairs of his ability to carry it through.

There are always in history vultures ready to swoop down when a form of thinking—reason, for instance—suffers a grave crisis that reveals its irremediable insufficiency. But no sooner have they pecked the bones clean than those same vultures cannot help starting afresh to rehash their old vulture ideas and their scavenger "philosophies." As vultures and hyenas feed on carrion, so certain manners of thinking start from the disasters that periodically befall the poor being called human.

It is not possible to ascertain the consistency of thinking by means of psychological investigation. Rather the order is inverse: because the nature of thinking is vaguely known, psychology is able to mark certain psychic phenomena as predominantly intellectual.[9] They are called thus because they play a part in the pursuit of thinking, and not the other way around.

Another screen obscuring the genuine phenomenon of thinking is provided by logic. Here the obscuring process consists in a reduction to an abstract pattern. Of the rich morphology of thinking, only one form is left, *logical* thinking, which is a thinking characterized by certain distinguishing features: identity

---

[8] We must not forget that all those intellectual functions that allegedly constitute thinking may also act of their own accord without and even against our will. Perception and imagination, even reasoning, are constantly and automatically at work in our mind. They are therefore not our doing, not *action*. The difference between an *action* and a mechanism lies in the intervention of the will and therewith of an intention and an end in view.

[9] This does not affect in the least the importance and interest of psychological research in itself.

with itself, avoidance of contradiction, exclusion of a third term between "true" and "false." Any thinking that fails to display these qualities, since it has fallen short of its standard, is not to be deemed genuine thinking. The obscuring effect caused in the course of two thousand years by this almost religious command to be logical is incalculable. It has divided the immense kingdom of the human intellect into two very unequal territories: on the one hand the most restricted world of the logical, on the other the negative domain of the illogical which has received little attention since nobody has quite known what to make of it. No distinction was made between logical and rational phenomena, and logic eventually became synonymous with reason. All this was inevitable and perfectly justified, because one believed that there actually exists a thinking that is wholly and unreservedly logical. With it, European man was convinced that he had at his disposal a procedure of rigorous stringency distinguished from the muddling ways of all other modes of thinking. But it so happens that we are now beginning to discover that no such logical thinking exists. The illusion vanished when the crude theory that for twenty-three centuries had borne the name of logic proved no longer sufficient. During the last three generations logic has suffered a fate that befell other great themes of science before it: it was actually put to the test. When a serious attempt was made to construe logic logically—in logistics, symbolic logic, mathematical logic —it appeared that this was impossible; that no concept is ultimately and strictly identical with itself; that no judgment can be guaranteed not to imply a contradiction; that there are judgments that are neither true nor false; that certain truths can be proved to be undemonstrable; in consequence, that there are illogical truths.[10] This very fact changes the picture completely. Logic that reveals itself to be pervaded by illogical elements loses its *emphatic aloofness from other forms of thinking*. Logi-

[10] About this point, "that there must always be undemonstrable mathematical truths," cf. William Van Orman Quine, *Mathematical Logic*, New York, W. W. Norton and Co., 1940.

cal thinking now turns out to be no thinking at all—indeed not, as there is no such thing as logical thinking—but only the idea of an imaginary thinking, a mere ideal, and a utopia misunderstanding itself. Aristotle's Logic is as unreal—and unreal for the same reasons—as Plato's Republic.

Theories like that of Lévy-Brühl's, who contrasts our so-called logical thinking with the "prelogical thinking" of primitive man, now appear entirely inappropriate. The discovery that our thinking is much less logical than we supposed has opened our eyes to the fact that primitive thinking is much more logical than we supposed. Instead of an absolute distinction singling out one form of thinking among all others that man has tried in the course of history, we now see continuity obtaining between all of them—or, which is the same, logical thinking, once it is recognized to be not the only representative of thinking, appears in its genuine shape, consenting of necessity to a few other principles besides those of identity, noncontradiction, and the excluded third. For I repeat: if thinking ultimately depended on the presence of these three attributes, we should have to admit that it never existed. And the fact is that in one way or another, willingly or reluctantly, with zest or sluggishly, man has always thought.

HISTORICAL CHARACTER OF COGNITION

But besides these two masks there is another denser one that hides the consistency of thinking from us. In both these cases we answered the question "What is thinking?" by adducing things that do not pretend to be themselves concrete, actual thinking. Psychology puts forward intellectual activities—that is, tools that provide the possibility of thinking. Logic is content to point at certain formal patterns of thinking that exhibit allegedly logical qualities. But what is called cognition or knowledge exercises an obscuring power so effective that it practically behaves like a synonym of thinking. In point of fact, cognizing is thinking—concrete, operative thinking in full execution. Neither mere intellectual activities—what the ancient called "faculties"—nor logical patterns are full-fledged instances of thinking. But cognition is. Here the error lies in assuming that the opposite also holds true, that all thinking is a cognitive act. Our next task, if we want to gain the open and chart a way toward the solution of the great problem, will therefore consist in telling apart these two traditionally associated terms.

The assumption is that man whenever he has set himself to thinking has done so with the same end in view: to ascertain what things are. This pursuit being called cognition, it would follow that thinking and cognizing are the same. And indeed, in drawing this inference informally and with a clear notion of the informal character of the assertion and of the comfortable inaccuracy of the terms implied, we have by no means fallen into error. The error only arises when the vague phrase "to ascertain what things are" inadvertently assumes its exact meaning. For it is not true that man has always proposed to discover the being of what surrounds him. Thus identification of thinking and cognition is due to a fallacy. The word cognition is employed in two meanings, one vague and one exact.

To know what to make of it all—the world and his own life—has ever mattered to man. When he feels sure about a thing, he will not trouble to start thinking but will quietly abide in whatever thought or idea he holds about it. In my terminology, an "idea in which man abides" is called a belief.[11] But when this belief fails him and he has nowhere to *abide*, he must do something to find out anew what to make of that particular thing. *Whatever* he then resorts to is thinking. There is no escape; man cannot help striving for certainty. This distinguishes him from animals and from gods. How, then, can we describe the operation man performs when thinking? Thinking may indeed take on many different forms. There is no one form man possesses

[11] Cf. the author's book *Ideas y creencias* (Ideas and Beliefs), Colección Austral, 1941.

once and for all that is "natural" to him and that, with more or less perfection, he has constantly practiced. The only thing he never lacks is the *need* of thinking; for he always lives in doubt of some sort. But the modes of satisfying this need—or rather the devices of endeavoring to do so, what may be called the techniques, stratagems, or *methods* of thinking—are in principle unlimited, and none is given to him, none is a "gift" with which he can forthwith reckon. Rather he must invent them and train himself to handle them, experimenting with them, trying out their possible scope and, in the end, always coming up against their limits. Nothing is more unfair than to credit human "nature"—our "nature," the sum and substance of that which is given to us and which we possess congenitally—with all those intellectual procedures the poor being called "man" has had to work out with toil and trouble in order to extract himself from the pit into which he fell by coming into existence.[12]

One, but *only one*, of these procedures is cognition in the strict sense of the word. Cognition is the attempt to solve the riddle of life by making intellectual mechanisms function in a formal way under the ultimate direction of concepts and their combinations in ratiocination. Surprisingly enough, it has always been taken for granted that man has felt at all times equally inclined to dedicate himself to this most peculiar occupation. The most summary reflection, however, discloses the fact that if man is to embark upon such a pursuit at least two presuppositions must be fulfilled. First, a belief must obtain that behind the confusion and chaos of the world as it appears to us there lies concealed a fixed and stable figure on which all changes depend and which, once revealed, gives a clue to what happens around us. This fixed and stable figure has, since the days of Greece, been called *being*. Cognition is ascertainment of the being of things in this strict sense of a "fixed and stable figure." The second implication without which conceptual pursuit of knowledge would be absurd is the belief that this *being*

[12] Cf. the author's book *Ensimismamiento y alteración* (Being Inside and Being Beside Oneself), Espasa Calpe, 1940.

is of a consistency akin to the natural human gift called intellect. Only when these two conditions are fulfilled does it make sense to hope that our *intellect* may serve to penetrate reality to the point of discovering its latent *being*.

Let us try to visualize the inner condition of a man who makes an effort to know. Supposing, for instance, he is intrigued by the unpredictable caprices of light phenomena. He mobilizes his intellectual devices and sets out seeking for an entity that when found will put him in a state of certainty concerning the nature of light. Seeking is a strange operation. In it we hunt for something which, in a certain way, we are already holding. When I try to pick out a red bead from among various beads of various colors I start with a red bead already in mind. In point of fact, I anticipate a red bead, and *that is why* I look for it. In the same way a man who begins to muse upon light phenomena anticipates (1) that in or, as it were, behind these phenomena there exists something which, once discovered, can restore him to a state of satisfaction and certainty regarding light, and (2) that this thing will let itself be captured through processes of reasoning. Otherwise there would be no point in having reason search for it. This something is the *being* of light, its fixed and stable behavior from which derive in a regular way the innumerable phenomena of light, so uncontrollable in their seeming disorder and intricate confusion. The fixity and stability of *being*, its always being what it is, endows it with the character of identity. As this character is proper to concepts also, *being* and thinking turn out to be of like consistency, and the laws that hold for concepts hold for *being*. Once we have found in the phenomenon of light this something immutable and stable, we call it the truth about light and assert this truth in propositions or theses such as: light is vibration, etc. Such propositions are the result of our cognitive pursuit.

But let us bear in mind that if these propositions result from our cognitive effort, there obtained before and thus without such effort—without cognition—a preconception that light, and things in general, is endowed with being. Without this *supposi-*

tion the intellectual process would not have got under way and would not have arrived at *propositions*. But calling this preconception a supposition must not be understood as conveying that it carries less conviction than the proposition. On the contrary, a man who sets out to know presupposes or supposes beforehand with radical conviction that there is being, and therefore searches for it to see what it is like.

But this means that cognition starts out with a perfectly determined opinion about the world—the opinion that things have being. And as this opinion is previous to any proof or reason and the presupposition of all proof or reasoning, we may safely maintain that it is nothing if not a belief and as such of the same kind as a religious faith.

Cognizing, we see, is more than "putting into action intellectual activities or psychic mechanisms which proceed from perception to abstraction." It is an occupation to which a man can dedicate himself *only* when holding the firm prerational belief that there is being. When he is in doubt as to what to make of this thing or that, or things in general, he has recourse to something beyond doubt, something meaning to him not a mere idea he happens to have conceived but reality itself: the being which, according to his deep belief, lies behind appearances. He exerts himself to know, not because he finds himself possessed of certain intellectual activities but because he lives in a most distinct belief which, far from being an abstract faculty of forming ideas, is itself an operative and concrete idea, an intellectual product, a doctrine. As there are no given and innate ideas, such a belief is not presented to man as a permanent constitutional gift appertaining to what since Aristotle has been called his nature. It is a state of mind at which *he has arrived* by a series of experiences in living, passing through successive trials and errors on his own account and with the co-operation of former generations and their tradition preserved by the collectivity in which he was born and reared. Or more simply, it happened to man that he arrived at the belief that reality has being because he had before held other beliefs—in the gods, for instance—the failure and downfall of which prepared him for this new one.

The foregoing considerations cannot but produce a radical change in our customary idea of cognition. From being considered an inborn faculty of man, and therefore permanent and inalienable, cognition comes to be recognized as a historical form evolved by human life as a result of certain previous experiences. This change of aspect is attained by simply taking into account the precognitive implication operating, as it were, at the back of cognition. We thus avoid the fallacy resulting from the ambiguous use of the word cognition, which sometimes denotes any mental effort to face the perplexities of life, and then again assumes its exact meaning of ascertainment of a supposed being which hides behind reality and which, owing to its identical consistency, may be grasped by concepts that are of the same kind. A concise description of the structure of cognition is enough to disclose its merely historical condition.

Moreover, in giving this description we come to realize that only in Greece and only for a few centuries did there exist a cognizing in the exact sense of the word. Only there and at that time was man engrossed in this pursuit without reserve, because only there and at that time did he live in the unshaken belief that reality consists in being, wholly and exclusively. All Hellenic thinking moved in the medium of this belief which molded Greek minds with the absolute power of pure faith. To the Greeks, cognition is that which yields definitive knowledge. Our empirical sciences they would not have regarded as cognition. For modern physics does not search for being. It contents itself with working out an imaginary, subjective pattern which allows us to take our bearings among appearances but which does not claim to be more than an approximation open at any time to corrections suggested by newly observed phenomena. Only that which is science of the immutable and therefore itself immutable was called cognition in Greece. The word denoted not intellectual manipulation of reality, as it does with us, but revelation of reality—*aletheia*.

No human achievement can be rightly understood without an analysis of the unquestioned beliefs that silently, invisibly, operate at the back of the human mind. Take Buddhism. We cannot understand it if we are not aware that Buddha starts as from something taken for granted, from the fact that the individual, since it is undying, is inescapably caught in the eternal chain of reincarnation. The sense of being doomed to immortality holds peculiar horrors; and Buddhism is nothing but the technique of a transcendental suicide that brings about the annihilation and dissolution of the fearfully imperishable individual soul in the universal and nonindividualized existence of nirvana.

As an example of a less intense but in its way not less effective belief let me cite Kepler who tells us by what mental procedures—through which states of mind—he came to discover his laws. Through his own testimony we know that he had a Pythagorean faith in the world's being ruled not only by mathematical relations but by very simple mathematical relations.

Surprisingly enough, no attempt has been made to analyze what reality looked like to Greek man before his mind reacted upon it in order to produce a philosophy. All deliberate and explicit philosophizing moves in the atmosphere of a "pre-philosophy," a conviction that remains mute because it stands the philosopher in the stead of "reality itself." Only an elucidation of this pre-philosophy—that is, of underlying and not yet rationalized beliefs—can explain the limitations of the articulate philosophy. Thus, for instance, Greek man of the age in which philosophy began—in Ionia, Samos, and Elea—lived in the radical belief that behind the apparent changes through which, like all human beings, he had to pick his way of life, there lies concealed an immutable reality—*physis* or Nature—from which according to strict rules the foreground changes emerge.

And this Nature, he believed, had *always been there*. The concept of the void was inconceivable to a Greek of that epoch. He started out from an unquestionably eternal reality, self-sustaining and not in need of a creator. It is these two attributes, eternity and immutability, which the Greeks expressed with the word "being" when using it in its full and genuine sense. An accidental world like the Christian universe, which, in order to exist, requires a creative act and therefore never ceases to bear the traces of its own previous nonexistence, would have filled the Greek with the same vital terror a Christian would experience if his God were taken from him.

We have inherited from Greece the idea of cognition. But we have not, at least not with sufficient integrity, inherited the belief in being or *natura rerum* that backs it. Hence the constant perplexities of the cognitive endeavor throughout Occidental history.

How did Greek man acquire such a belief in being and such a faith in Nature? This is a problem of high rank, but one that has never been studied or even posed. As there was, in the Greek mind, no question about this belief, there was no question either about its implication that cognition—the capture of being—constituted a natural, congenital function of man. But we have been left with the latter conviction minus the faith on which it was based. Thus the problem now comes walking up to us on its own feet: why did Greek man find himself with the "Great Faith" in the being of things which is the presupposition of cognition proper?

Persians, Assyrians, Hebrews were no "cognizers." They believed that reality is identical with God. But God, a true God, has no stable and fixed consistency; he is pure will, absolute, unlimited, and arbitrary. A man who believes truly, and not with subterfuges and compromises, and watering the strong wine of such belief, that *what is there* is God and that therefore all the rest that seems to be there does not exist strictly speaking but flows out of the indomitable will of God—a man who so believes can obviously not believe that things possess being, consistency of their own and therefore not only exist but in existing have a fixed and determined consistency. To a true believer in God it could not possibly occur that his intellect might be of any avail in his intercourse with things. He feels himself inexorably thrown upon the mercy of God, the one decisive reality. What is to befall him and his people depends on the will and the inscrutable and inescapable decrees of God. If such a man is assailed by grave doubts about certain orders of his life, he will do something indeed, he will not remain idle. But what will he do? Reason? that is, analyze, compare, infer, prove, conclude? By no means. He will pray, pray to God that he may be enlightened and given certainty. Praying is a form and a technique of thinking. For the believer in God there is no other means of knowing than to entreat God that he reveal his will to him and, when God hears his prayer and chooses him among the rest, to communicate God's will to his people by abolishing all ideas of his own and making himself the organ of God and the mouthpiece of the Almighty. His saying has nothing in common with the *logos* of reason; it is not *aletheia*—discovery of hidden being which is there once and for all. Rather he says today what, according to God's resolve and decree, is to be tomorrow; his saying is presage inspired by God, prophecy. And since God's will is irrevocable, he will speak with a humble and absolute confidence in that secret divine voice which is at once free and certain, decision and promise. What he speaks is not the *logos* of truth: A *is* B. It is the *amen* of faith: *so shall it be.* For such a man reality has the tense not of the present indicative but of the future. What he conveys is a "will be" not an "is." His world is in a state of constant creation; it is what God, at each moment, wills it to be.

Amen, 'emunah, is the Hebrew word for "truth." [13] The con-

---

[13] Cf. the rectoral address of Hans Freiherr von Sodden, *Was ist Wahrheit?,* 1927. The noun *'emunah*—*amen* is a verb form—derives from a root whose primary meaning is "firm," "sure," but chiefly with reference to the personal sphere, as, for instance, in a firm promise or a firm friendship. Here an orientation toward the future enters—that the friend *will* be found loyal, that the promise *will* be kept—through which the noun *'emunah* comes to denote confidence. That from "confidence" it should then have passed to designate "truth" shows how strongly the Hebrews—like the Assyrians and the Persians—felt themselves confronted not with being or Nature but with an absolute will transcending all being—ἐπέκεινα τῆς οὐσίας, to quote Plato who mediatized and annulled this being.

It is worth noticing that the most technical expression Aristotle sees himself compelled to use for denoting the "substance" of a thing, and therewith the most authentic being, is his extravagant term—a term in the form of a whole sentence that must be understood as a name—τὸ τί ἦν εἶναι or "a-thing-being-what-it-

trast between Greek *aletheia* and Hebrew *'emunah* is so striking that the clash between the two cannot fail to open our eyes
to the merely historical character of cognition. This confronta-
tion may then be used for clarifying finer points. It will allow
us to view from within, with an intimacy heretofore unobtain-
able, other earlier modes of thinking that have remained incomprehensible to modern man, as, for instance, those operative in
mythology, magic, "wisdom" or "experience of life."

With this we have achieved a few things of considerable import. Cognition now appears not as an absolute reality to which
man is committed forever and ever but as a pure historical
phenomenon; not as a "natural" and therefore inevitable occupation of man but as one "form of life" invented and developed in the course of history by way of answer to certain experiences and liable to be dropped in view of others.

Furthermore, from this standpoint cognition ceases to be a
utopia and appears in its own concrete and relative consistency.
This enables us to treat of it historically. We can ask why man
embarked upon precisely this occupation, and why in Greece
and nowhere else cognition came fully into its own, or, to put
it differently, why the Greeks alone believed truly and unreservedly in the possibility of cognizing. Starting from that plenary
and purest form of cognition in Greece we may trace through
subsequent history down to our day the *progressive deteriora-
tion of the idea (and the occupation) of cognizing.* In this way

---

was." To a Greek, as I said before, being has the present tense; but looked at
very closely, it turns out to be standing in the past. Given the Greek idea of
being, such a chronological perspective is inevitable. The reality *now* standing
before me—what is present—is partly accidental, a pseudo being. This pseudo
being is only now, and was not before. It is the result of a temporary cause, of
chance. But behind it lies also *now*—that is, in the present—the true being or
the substance. And the substance is what it is now *because* it already was this
before, in an indefinite past, always. True being is essentially a having-been-
before, a *próteron*. That is why it is called principium, *arché*, something ancient.
And the science of being turns out to be—archaeology. No wonder that Aristotle
got considerably entangled when dealing with the origin of forms—a problem
which, in the nineteenth century, was to give rise to an epic controversy between
the dull and gentle Zeller and the impetuous firebrand Brentano.

the present grave crisis of reason loses, of itself, the aspect of a sudden, unprecedented cataclysm.

Last and most important, all this allows us to deal with the present crisis by placing ourselves outside it. If cognition were something man had done and were to go on doing forever, this crisis would mean a crisis for man himself. But once cognition is revealed as just one historical form of human life, it may be assumed that man has had before and will have hereafter other equally normal ways of facing the enigma of his life and escaping from doubt into certainty. Thus we obtain, for the first time, a philosophy aware of its own end and foreseeing further forms of human reaction destined to supersede it.

To believe that the present crisis of the intellect can be solved by any less radical revision of traditional notions would be idle. And these are no vague problems. Right now we may, for instance, predict that as soon as physics, the exemplary science of the Western world, returns from the fray to tranquil reflection upon itself, there will emerge a "critique of physical reason" in which cognition will appear in an entirely new light.

As a result of the foregoing distinctions, thinking now comes into full view unobscured by the particular forms of which it allows. Behind these forms we may now watch it at work, creating those of the past and ever abandoning yesterday's for those of tomorrow. From this standpoint we may divine, not without a sense of awe, what is not yet there, the germinating future of the human intellect.

The characterization given in the preceding paragraphs of cognition as a historical entity cannot even claim to convey as much as a schematic outline. It does not aspire to furnish more than a paradigm in which the special case of cognition is subjected to an operation of general import which, under the title of historical reason, has for these past years been the main subject of my philosophical work. My aim is to follow into its ultimate consequences the observation that the specifically human reality—man's life—is of historical consistency. Such an undertaking requires that all concepts referring to the integral phenomenon of human life be "denaturalized" and subjected to a process of "historification." Whatever man is he is not once and for all; he has one day *come to be thus* and will one day *cease to be thus.* Permanence in the forms of human life is an optical illusion from which we suffer, thanks to a certain crudeness of concepts. Ideas that hold only when applied abstractly to those forms are used as if they were concrete and capable of genuinely representing reality.

Thus we have distinguished in the concept of cognition two different values. It may denote any attempt made by man to adjust himself intellectually to his environment. This is an abstract concept made up of abstract constituents: abstract man, an environment no less abstract, the abstract necessity of adjustment between the two, and the notion of a likewise abstract intellectual activity. No doubt, every concrete man—and that means man *always*—is doing something wherein these components are present, but he is *never* doing something that consists of these components *only.* To begin with, he is not *man* but *a man* born at a definite date and formed by a definite tradition out of which he acts as he does. Nor is his environment simply an environment. It is a system, determined by the tradition into which he was born, of difficulties and facilities for his particular life: for instance, his stock aspirations or, which is the same, his idea of "happiness" and his stock techniques. Finally, the intellect is no fixed entity. Its reality and concrete appearance—reality is always and exclusively concrete—varies incessantly in the course of history with the varying use it is put to and the varying education—or "gymnastics"—it is subjected to. Primitive man thought *less* logically than Poincaré or Hilbert not because his intellect was constitutively illogical or prelogical but because he did not as deliberately and constantly aspire to be logical as did these two men who were born into an unbroken logical tradition of twenty-six centuries.

The abstract concept of cognition is therefore like an algebraic expression which in order to represent reality requires its blank spots (*Leerstellen*) to be filled out by concrete numbers denoting distances, frequencies, forces. When the vacancies in the abstract concept are filled out with concrete ideas the radical diversity of actions jumbled up under the general denomination of cognition comes into view, and we are faced with the necessity of attaching the term to one of them or, at most, to a group of such actions as have most elements in common.

This would then be the concrete concept of cognition, whereas the term thinking ought to be set aside for signifying the abstract idea of man's intellectual adjustment to his environment. But in assigning this meaning to it we pledge ourselves not to conceive it as anything but an algebraic formula of a human doing, the actual values of which must be determined historically. And that implies nothing less than the fact that every concept claiming to represent human reality carries a date inside or, which is the same, that every concept referring to specifically human life is a function of historical time.

The type of investigation we have here suggested in connection with cognition ought to be carried through in the same way for the benefit of poetry, law, language, religion, "wisdom" or experience of life, etc. To use the name poetry indiscriminately for what a Greek of the seventh century heard in Homer's verses and for one of Musset's *Nuits* really means confounding things too lightheartedly. In the same way the word religion becomes ambiguous when it denotes simultaneously two such heterogeneous things as Christianity and the beliefs, feelings, and actions of a Roman of the first Punic War in his intercourse with his gods—or even, within Christianity, the Christianity of St. Augustine and that of Cardinal Newman.[14]

Whoever aspires to understand man—that eternal tramp, a thing essentially *on the road*—must throw overboard all immobile concepts and learn to think in ever-shifting terms.

---

[14] Catholicism, in contrast with Protestantism, is characterized by a keen consciousness of the historical dimension inherent in religion notwithstanding its perpetuity.

APPENDIX

Owing to reasons which, when advanced here laconically, would seem abstract to the reader, phenomenology, not differing in this from the philosophies preceding it, is a "naïve or unjustified philosophy." These adjectives must not be understood as carrying a valuation. They imply no disrespect or disparagement but simply express an intrinsic feature of those philosophies. I call a philosophy naïve or unjustified when it leaves outside its doctrinal body the motives from which it springs—in other words when it fails to recognize as a constitutive part of itself the facts that prompted its creation. Philosophy is wont to begin abruptly as a series of theses on reality or on the principles of truth, without explaining *philosophically* why in the world it should be needful to make such statements on reality or on truth.

The logical necessity or, which is the same, the truth of those theses is expounded to us. But we are left wondering whether and to what degree it is necessary to go to the trouble of enunciating them. Every human occupation aspires to justify itself not only before other people but in the eyes of him who is absorbed in it. It is not so much that this *ought* to be done but that it is done, wittingly or unwittingly. And when the occupation, as in the case of philosophy, pretends to be concerned with the universe—that is, to be all inclusive—justification has no place organically to accommodate itself except in the very body of the philosophical doctrine as one of its constitutive parts. Geometry and physics are exempt from this obligation because special sciences are deliberately naïve. That is their virtue and their limitation. In delimiting their field, they forgo—at least in principle—all obtrusive and aggressive intentions. If you are not interested in them, they leave you alone. I speak of the sciences themselves, not of the men of science.[15] But philosophy carries

[15] In the beginning of the twentieth century, physicists and natural scientists still behaved aggressively, exercising what I used to call the "terror of labora-

inside itself an inalienable violence which stands in marked contrast to the peaceful disposition developed by the philosophical guild after their first steps in history. The courtesy and euphemism practiced by philosophers may tend to hide this, but for the last twenty-six centuries philosophy itself, as it cannot warp its substance and cease being what it is, has been implying a constant implacable insult. The existence of philosophy in the world signifies, tacitly or blatantly, that a living being who has none is little better than a brute. Wherever in this sublunary world philosophy is absent, there reigns somnambulism; animals are characterized by their sleepwalking existence. And be it understood, it is not I who say this—in fact, my own philosophy may in this terrible point introduce a certain correction—but this has been implicitly said all along by the very fact of "philosophy." After the heroic age of philosophy in Ionia and Magna Graecia, in Miletus and Elea, philosophers contrived to sugar-coat the insult. In the *Apology* Socrates says: "A life without philosophy is not livable for man." And in Aristotle we read: "All the other sciences which are not philosophy are more necessary, but none is more important than philosophy." Deduct the euphemism, and you are left with the insult.

An occupation of such aggressively exigent ways stands in intrinsic need of justification. Else its claim would remain a mere arrogant, impotent gesture, and it would be but another form of sleepwalking. Only if men cannot help making philosophy and being philosophers can the existence of both be borne with. And, I repeat, not for reasons of social intercourse, not in order to assert itself against the hostile opinion of other people, but because otherwise it would be meaningless to itself, must philosophy include in its own anatomy the organ of its own justification. Nor do such considerations suffice as may be found by way of *preambula fidei* or prologue in the beginning of philosophical treatises. Even in the eyes of their writer such observations are not yet philosophy but an informal preliminary

tories." But this attitude was abandoned soon after, and today it appears only here and there as a surviving fossil.

elucidation, something like a proffered spoon to take in the philosophy. In the first book of Aristotle's *Metaphysics*, for example, an explanation is given of why one philosophizes. But this explanation manifestly remains outside the philosophy proper. It does not affect the content of Aristotle's philosophical thesis and does not influence his doctrine—whereas from the justification I demand must derive, as from a principle, the ideas of the philosophical system itself. Or to state this in its turn as a thesis: The justification of a philosophy is its first principle. What impels man to philosophize forms part of the philosophical theory itself.

I will give a minor example, reserving for another occasion a somewhat detailed exposition of another and monumental one.[16] In the beginning of the *Essay Concerning Human Understanding* Locke says that our task in this world is not to know all things but only to know those relevant to our conduct.

The philosophical content of this pronouncement is usually

---

[16] The monumental example is the *Discours de la méthode*. The *Discourse on Method*—opening theme of the symphony of modern thinking—is an autobiography. In it Descartes tells us which experiences of his life led to the discovery of his philosophy. It might have aroused a little more surprise that a whole epoch of human thinking—and the most glorious save for the great centuries in Greece —should have begun with the memoirs of a personal life. That Descartes considered as philosophy only a certain theoretical result to which his experiences had led is no sufficient reason for us not to ask systematically for the connection between that result and those experiences. Defining this connection is tantamount to understanding the absolute human fact that is the *Discourse*. If philology were what it ought to be—the science of reading—it should have observed of its own accord, apart from any philosophical considerations, that these allegedly philosophical theses on method are meaningless unless they are understood as actually emerging from the experiences that had arisen in the man Descartes, experiences that are not individual anecdotes but a precipitation left by the whole of European history.

However, to drop these assertions as I do here, not only by the way but in full career, is disheartening because "precipitation of the whole of European history" must sound like a vague phrase whereas it is a most concrete notion revealed and confirmed, without the slightest strain, by every word of the *Discourse*. For many years I have been preparing in my seminars at the University of Madrid a commentary on the illustrious Cartesian text. The commentaries we have are few and unsatisfactory, although that by Gilson is respectable through its erudite accumulation of facts which may profit an interpretation of deeper draft. My intention to read my paper in 1937 before the Paris congress celebrating the three hundredth anniversary of the publication of Descartes' book was barred by all too notorious historical events.

seen in its negative and limitative signification which implies a reduction of the field of knowledge. "Relevant to conduct" functions as a criterion indicating all those themes of knowledge that bear this name by rights and about which it makes sense to reflect—that is, to philosophize. But in drawing this line, philosophy behaves like a special science which may indeed be content to declare: I will be concerned with spacial relations only—geometry; or: I will be concerned with directly or indirectly measurable phenomena only—physics; save that in the case of special sciences such limitation is sufficiently precise, and that its precision serves as a practical substitute for justification.

The true justification of modern physics lies in its technical application. And modern mathematics, as an ingredient of physics, benefits by this justification; whereas ancient mathematics stood justified on the strength of its metaphysical dignity. It must be borne in mind that, immediately or mediately, all ancient mathematics is of Pythagorean tradition.

But the declaration that only what concerns conduct must be regarded as knowledge proper supplies but a vague indication which guarantees nothing and leaves philosophy in a situation worse than that of those other sciences. Moreover, Locke is satisfied with advancing his proposition and neither founds nor analyzes it. To him it is a "topic" in the concise sense of the Aristotelian term: an opinion which strictly speaking is no "truth" and from which no "truths" can be derived. It is simply what-people-think, public opinion, *endoxa*.

Suppose, now, instead of leaving this enunciation at the noncommittal threshold of philosophy, as Locke did, we take it philosophically seriously—that is, we resolve to state it as the great primary thesis of philosophy. This obviously entails the duty of proving it, whatever regimen of proof it may admit or stand in need of. *Ipso facto* Locke's limp phrase therewith acquires vigor and urgency and reveals that its philosophical significance lies in its positive rather than in its negative meaning. Now, to Locke himself his assertion, as he actually depended on it for making his philosophy, possessed *in fact* this positive meaning. What traditionally bore the name philosophy did not satisfy him. He did not *formulate* his opinion as a thesis but he *practiced* it as such. It is a thesis in the form of action signifying nothing less than that knowledge is not something substantive in its own right but a function of human life, and that life in its turn is a task. Or, in a different order, (1) our existence in the world is a task; (2) this task consists not so much in cognizing as in "conducting ourselves"; (3) knowledge is a task in so far as it is required by "conduct." Those are three fundamental philosophical principles which Locke's philosophy was unaware of but which, operating inside it, were instrumental in its creation. And in this implied philosophy that was left standing before the door, the official Lockean doctrine would, to boot, have found its justification.

If Husserl in making phenomenology—which to him was the true philosophy—had paused in his advance to reflect on the course his mind had taken up to that point in which, *to his judgment,* his formal doctrine evolved, he would have observed that this formal doctrine was inseparable from nondoctrinal motives in which it originated and *on which it depended.* Man makes philosophy for the sake of certain pre-theoretical and a-theoretical needs and conveniences. These needs and conveniences are not vague but precise, and they *condition most determinately the intellectual exercise* called reason. There is a significant resemblance between the opening sentences of Locke's *Essay* and the passage from Husserl's *Formal and Transcendental Logic* quoted earlier.[17] As with Locke knowledge is a function of life, so with Husserl reason is a "function of humanity," humanity being nothing if not the totality of men past and present. But neither Locke nor Husserl made this point seriously.

Phenomenology, which lays claim to being the supreme expression of reason, has the formal character of an independent activity and not of a function of life; it is knowledge for the

[17] Cf. p. 55.

sake of knowledge. In the analysis and definition of reason given by Husserl in *Formal and Transcendental Logic,* the themes of humanity, life, and the functional character of reason are not and indeed could not be taken up again. They remain extrinsic and informal. That promised "radical reflection" on what is knowledge does not come forth, and if it did I much doubt that it could have attained a sufficient degree of radicalism. It was too late for that. The sphere of absolute reality—Husserl's *reine Erlebnisse* (pure experiences)—has, in spite of its juicy name, nothing to do with life; it is, strictly speaking, the opposite of life. The phenomenological attitude is diametrically opposed to the attitude that I call living reason.

Husserl, like all idealistic philosophers of whom he is the last representative, begins with affirming as the basic fact of maximum evidence that reality constitutes itself in *consciousness of* reality—for instance, in *consciousness of* (the real world) which consists principally in the conscious acts called perceptions. The actual reality of this world is relative—namely, relative to this *consciousness of* it that I have. But as reality precludes relativity, this means that the reality of the world, being relative to *consciousness of* it, is problematic, and only my *consciousness of* (the reality of the world) has absolute reality. The reality of my *consciousness of* something is relative to itself; for according to Husserl and all idealism, consciousness is conscious of itself, or in other words, it is immediate to itself.[18] But to be relative to oneself is tantamount to being absolute.

Now, if *consciousness of* is the absolute reality and as such the starting point of philosophy, philosophy would start from a reality in which the subject—I—exists enclosed within itself, within its mental acts and states. But such existence in the form of *being enclosed in oneself* is the opposite of what we call *living.* Living means *reaching out of* oneself, devoted, ontologically, to what is *other*—be it called world or circumstances.

[18] For all this, cf. the article by León Dujovne, "Ortega y Gasset and Historical Reason," *La Nación,* December, 1940, in which an excellent summary is given of my fundamental criticism of idealism as I expounded it in a course of lectures in Buenos Aires.

To start from life as the primary and absolute fact is to recognize that *consciousness of* is solely an idea, a more or less justified and plausible one, but no more than an idea which we have discovered or invented in the process of living and for motives arising from this our living. Living reason starts from no idea and hence is not idealism.

Husserl proposes to arrive at the roots (we are promised "radical reflection") of knowledge by way of phenomenological analysis. He anticipates—how can he help it?—that these roots are pre-theoretical, let us vaguely say "vital." But since he comes upon all this in the process of philosophizing and making phenomenology, and since phenomenology has not justified and founded itself, the whole consideration remains hanging in the air.[19]

---

[19] In his *Formal and Transcendental Logic* Husserl, with a last supreme effort, expounded his "genetic phenomenology." This genetic phenomenology through which he sought to come in touch with the pre-theoretical reality which is "life" cannot react upon general phenomenology of which it is only a component part. Husserl died without publishing any concrete investigation on genetic phenomenology. He but put forth a summary program. It is to be hoped that Dr. Fink, his pupil and scientific executor, will publish the bulk of manuscript he left behind. Among them must be investigations dealing with these problems. At any rate, it seems to me that it ought to be possible without too much difficulty to determine precisely how far genetic phenomenology carries and what is its essential limit in dealing with the great problem of the "genesis of reason."
While reading the proofs of this essay, I happened to see that in 1935 Husserl gave a course of lectures at the University of Prague under the title "Crisis of the European Sciences and Transcendental Phenomenology," the beginning of which was published in the journal *Philosophia*, vol. I, 1936, Belgrade. In it the great philosopher gives a more detailed exposition of the ideas contained in the passage quoted above. We would therefore seem to have been mistaken in calling that passage unique in Husserl's intellectual style. In fact, we were not. The article in *Philosophia* was doubtless agreed on with Husserl in conversations, and ideas from his manuscripts were used in it. But the work—the last Husserl would have published in his lifetime—was obviously put into writing not by him but by Dr. Fink, whose style—of writing and thinking—is manifest throughout the text. Not only does the style differ from Husserl's but in this study phenomenology jumps to views that could never have organically grown from it. Personally, I am much gratified by this leap of phenomenological doctrine which means nothing less than a recourse to "historical reason." I should, however, like to state that my essay "History as a System," published in 1935, precedes those pages in *Philosophia* as well as their continuation in *Revue Internationale de Philosophie*, Brussels, 1939, where explicit mention is made of *Vernunft in der Geschichte* (reason in history).

Prologue

TO A

History

OF

Philosophy

Θεωροῦν . . . . ἐπίδοσις εἰς αὐτό

(Aristotle *On the Soul* II, 5, 417b, 5)

Contents

EPOCHS WITHOUT SPLENDOR

BESIDE epochs of splendor, there are in the history of philosophy epochs of dimmer light which always were, and in a way continue to be, the stepchildren of investigation. Some of them are called epochs of transition, others epochs of decline —names that intimate that they are periods of lesser philosophical production. But both these qualifications are inadequate. In history all is transition, so much so in fact that we may well define history as the science of transitions. Decadence, on the other hand, even when pronounced as a diagnosis and not as an insult, is too narrow a term. In so-called decadent periods some things decay, but others germinate. Both terms should therefore be used with a grain of caution. Instead of describing the period in question by its intrinsic characteristics, by features of life as it was then lived, they merely convey our valuation which, of necessity, remains external and alien to the reality at issue.

There have been times, no doubt, when people felt that they were living between a great past gone down and a great future yet to come. They may themselves have talked of their painfully suspended state as of a transition. But even in this extreme case those people merely expressed the idea they were holding of themselves. The historian must take note of it, for their opinion about themselves, even if it was wrong (which has occasionally happened), belongs to the historical reality with which he is concerned. But he must not accept it as title or definition of a historical era.

For further proof of the inadequacy of the term "transition" we need only point out that it is a concept of generic character and therefore applies to many entirely different periods. In fine, we should be aware of how little we are saying when we speak of transition or decline. Instead of using these terms like

apparatuses that can, by just functioning automatically, illuminate for us a piece of the past, let us regard them as an invitation to ascertain the strange, concrete forms that life has
taken on in various ages under the abstract signs of "transition"
and "decline."

The negative character of these two concepts must not let us
forget that every epoch is positive, that all life implies its own
affirmation, that mankind has at no time committed suicide.
And the ultimate task of the historian consists in discovering
even in the grimmest times such gratifying motives as induced
people to live on. Life in epochs of transition is not lived as
though it were in transition to another epoch; it is resolutely
established in its own time, no less so than life in most consolidated periods. For, vice versa, every time has had its non-
conformists, individuals or groups who preferred—or *believed*
they preferred—to their own age some other era, past or to
come. We must not confuse the phenomenon here in question
with the fact that in certain epochs people believed themselves
to be inordinately unhappy.

History of philosophy as a science is one of the most recent
disciplines. In fact, it is less than a hundred years old. During
the second half of the last century historians of philosophy had
to dedicate themselves to the most obvious task, that of reconstructing in first approximation the thought of the great figures
in philosophy. It was then that the first systematic studies in
Plato, Aristotle, Descartes, Leibnitz, Kant were made. Fichte,
Schelling, Hegel remained unknown for another twenty years;
and only in our days have we begun to study Spinoza.

But as a study of mountain peaks does not make an orography,
so these studies do not yet add up to a history of philosophy.
The peak calls for the valley.

Our picture of the past still looks somewhat like an Alpine
scene on a foggy day. High above us we see the pinnacles of the
loftiest ranges floating disconnected, imponderous, and unreal
over the soft chaos of the fog. There may appear indistinctly in
the shrouding haze one or another spectral physiognomy, but

we cannot see how the proud mountains rise from the ground and how the valleys connect them. And thus the main thing is missing: the geological structure of the towering ranges of philosophy.

In my opinion, history of philosophy cannot advance and establish itself in accordance with the promise contained in its name until we fill the gaps of knowledge that open like precipices between the great and noble periods of philosophical thought. It is the study of the twilight periods which is urgently needed.

Our lack of knowledge of these periods differs for different periods in character and in degree. Let us here describe it, if only through a brief example.

After Aristotle, obscurity already sets in. We have the three great philosophical systems of the "decline" of antiquity: stoicism, epicureanism, skepticism. It is not that no research on them has been done, on stoicism in particular. But the work can compare neither in volume nor in weight with the intense cultivation from which Plato and Aristotle have benefited. As it is, we have but a hazy notion of those great movements of the classical mind which, though doubtless less valuable as systems of conceptual technique than the first Academy and the Peripatetic School, have, however, exerted by far the greater influence in history. Never has a philosophy given more effective support to an empire than did stoicism to the mighty reign of the Antonines.[1] Moreover, in the lap of those philosophies, the ancient world came to its end and the new peoples of Europe were born. For Christianity was, in its early stages, pervaded to the very core of its still shapeless, shifting mass by the theology and the ethics of the stoics. And again in the times of the Renaissance these three philosophies, behind a superficial revival of neo-Platonic influence, transmitted the sap of ancient thinking to those new minds that inaugurated the modern age. Like three fairy godmothers, stoicism, epicureanism, and skep-

[1] Cf. M. I. Rostovtzeff, *The Social and Economic History of the Roman Empire, op. cit.*, I, ch. 4.

ticism hovered around the cradle of Descartes' philosophy and therewith of all classical European rationalism.

Thus we are confronted with the amazing fact that at their very emergence these three philosophies of "decline" dislodged Platonic-Aristotelian idealism from its predominance over the several intellectual groups of Greece, *although* to our mind they are the coarser philosophies. But this sweeping triumph of a rugged philosophy like stoicism over such marvels of precision and penetration as the systems of Plato and Aristotle is not only surprising in itself; it also sets us wondering what had become of the works of Aristotle after Aristotle's death. Another amazing fact: they vanished almost immediately. As early as fifty years after Aristotle's death, nobody any longer understood his pragmatic books which, for that reason, were rarely copied and have come down to us by a mere stroke of luck. People continued reading his dialogues, the *popular* and literary ("exoteric") part of his work. But it was not until the beginning of the first century B.C. that the technical works of Aristotle were rediscovered and studied again,[2] and not till well into the Middle Ages that they became a normal possession of educated people.

Zeno the Stoic was born in 320 B.C., two years after Aristotle's death. In his theories he still makes use of scraps from the Peripatetic system; to what extent and in what way have not yet been studied. But this appropriation does not affect the general outline of stoicism, which is not only another doctrine but a sudden drop in the level of the intellectual endeavor theretofore called philosophy. Historians of philosophy give little sign of being impressed by such a change. With the greatest of ease they propound Plato's and Aristotle's subtle idealism and then go on explaining stoic "materialism"—which, by the way, should not be called materialism; let us say "corporealism." But here lies a problem. What happened to Greek man in such sweep-

---

[2] Recalling his days of study in Greece, Cicero assures us *"quod quidem sum minime admiratus, eum philosophum rhetori non esse cognitum qui ab ipsis philosophis praeter admodum paucos ignoretur"* (*De topicis* I).

ing passage from Aristotle's pure "form" to the *pneuma* and *logos spermaticus* which are at once idea and body? We do not know. Though during the last twenty years this whole maze of problems [3] has begun to be explored, we are still groping in the dark.

No study has yet been made of the preliminary problem which, once solved, would allow us to decipher the hieroglyphs of stoicism: how it comes to pass that after Aristotle the meaning and style of philosophizing change so fundamentally that not only does stoicism differ from Aristotelism as one doctrine from another, but that the intellectual pursuit "philosophy" itself undergoes profound changes as to its aim, its presuppositions, its form of expression, and its methods. Here we come upon another untouched subject: to give precise and distinct account of this new occupation of Greek intellectuals which, though it continues to bear the old name of philosophy, is far removed from the kind of thinking Plato and Aristotle had done.

Elucidation of these problems may even have a retroactive effect on our knowledge of Plato and Aristotle. For in the process of, and owing to, the trivialization of the philosophical quest, there may have become manifest in stoicism certain characteristics of all Greek philosophy which in Plato and Aristotle reach us obscured by other splendors. And thus we may discover that our present picture of Platonism and Aristotelism is but an abstract aspect cut out from the integral reality of their philosophies and rendering only such traits as are akin to our own way of thinking.

There is, for instance, strong evidence for our having unduly neglected what *persisted* of religious elements in those two systems. Not that there can be any doubt that philosophy was *distinguished* from religion as a thing *sui generis;* but we should have recognized that religion, nonetheless, continued to be a factor of great moment in Plato and Aristotle. No history of philosophy that I know of has taken seriously the idea—so mo-

---

[3] For the same has happened with stoic "epistemology," whose central notion, the φαντασία καταληπτική, continues to be as much of a puzzle as ever.

mentous in Plato—that philosophizing is an *homoiosis thou
theou*, an imitation of God in the same sense in which Thomas à
Kempis speaks of *Imitatio Christi*. Yet we find this idea pronounced in solemn sentences in the tenth book of the *Niko-
machean Ethics* and the twelfth of the *Metaphysics* where Aristotelian philosophy culminates.

For all these reasons it would indeed seem indispensable
for us to possess sufficiently clear insight into historical phenomena of such caliber. But neither have epicureanism, stoicism, or skepticism received the study that their long history
deserves, nor are the studies dedicated to them what they ought
to be. It is no excuse that the books of the great heads of those
schools have not come down to us. The fragments extant are
considerable enough to allow of a fruitful work of reconstruc-
tive combination.[4]

We have come upon an example of the pernicious influence
exercised by a conventional historical conception like "epochs
of transition and decline." In fact, studies in Plato and Aristotle
are ready to go to any length to make the two philosophers
acceptable to us—that is, to make us see how very right Plato
and Aristotle were in thinking as they thought. Such efforts frequently overstep the mark, making the two Greek masters
appear like contemporaries of ours.[5]

Two motives may conceivably have led historians to bestow
upon the two ancient philosophers such excessive closeness to
modern man. The first is a kind of bigotry that has not yet been
completely eliminated from Latin and Greek philology. This
bigotry, which is neither worship nor enthusiasm but a silly

[4] A good instance of such investigation, although because of certain defects of
method the result turns out to be unsatisfactory, is the work in which Reinhardt
has tried to reconstruct the ideas of Poseidonios, the last great scientific thinker
of antiquity. Cf. Karl Reinhardt, *Poseidonios*, München, Beck, 1921, and *Kosmos
und Sympathie*, München, Beck, 1926.

[5] An extreme case of such lack of proportion is the research centering on Plato
by my two teachers Cohen and Natorp. According to them, Plato said approximately the same as Kant, and Kant as Natorp and Cohen. Their work has, nonetheless, illuminated many points in Plato's philosophy and marks, restored to a
more cautious perspective, a considerable progress.

variation of both, exalts the "classical" thinker above the level of history, and instead of trying simply and honestly to understand him as he is—a man among men, and that always means a *pauvre homme*—treats of him with the firm decision to admire, anticipating in his work imaginary perfections to which the texts are willy-nilly adapted. In this way the time-honored work is committed to assuming validity for all times. No wonder that the most elemental features of Platonic and Aristotelian thought remain unexplained. Why should they be explained, since they are considered exemplary? Thus the disgraceful situation arises that we do not yet know what the Platonic *dialogue* or Aristotle's *pragmateia* means as a literary form, a *genus dicendi*.

The second motive for making those great thinkers appear easier of access than they really are is more reasonable, though not altogether so. Philosophical problems contain an *abstract* kernel that has changed little from Heraclitus and Parmenides to our days.[6] The contemporary philosopher, pondering over the central questions of philosophy and gaining new insight, compares notes with the ancients and throws new light upon that comparatively invariant nucleus of problems. That is what Kant meant when he said that it is possible to understand Plato better than Plato understood himself. But Kant's remark only serves to reveal that the interest and the point of view of the systematic philosopher are not those of the historian. The latter must beware lest he understand Plato better than Plato understood himself. He has done much when he understands Plato as Plato understood himself. The one thing he must add is an elucidation of the fundamental conditions that determined Plato's scope but that Plato did not see because they were the very light by which he saw everything else.

The kind of adoration inflicted upon those two princes of philosophy has, with its dazzling effect, so incapacitated us for seeing them in their exact, magnificent historical form that what we now need most is to *estrange* and remove them from us, to emphasize their distance in time, and to let ourselves be

[6] For the meaning of this apparent immutability see p. 100.

overcome by the impression of how different in human ways, how altogether exotic, they are to us. Thus and only thus may we be able to come to a clear understanding of certain fundamental questions in their work which up to now have baffled all efforts.

On the other hand, no similar attempts have been made to mitigate the remoteness of the stoics, the epicureans, the skeptics, or representatives of any other lesser periods in the continuity of philosophy. They have been left too much at a distance, and thus remain debarred from any living, effective communication with us. This failure, combined with the opposite mistake which we have commented on above, imparts to the picture our historians are drawing of past philosophy a double perspective that would be unbearable in the humblest painting.[7]

BRIEF DIGRESSION ON THE "HISTORICAL SENSE"

It is the mission of history to make our fellow beings acceptable to us. For, queer though it sounds, they are not so. My neighbor is essentially an offense to me—an "outrage" in the

---

[7] Another persistent defect in the customary way of writing the history of philosophy is disregard of the history of science. Since Descartes, there has been a constant close connection between the *philosophia prima* and the sciences. Thus the philosophical thinking proper of roughly the last three centuries can be safely expounded without special attention to scientific research. In the first place, modern philosophy is, from the outset, charged with science, and anticipates in itself the world picture of science—mathematics, physics, biology. Second, from Descartes till very recently, science remained essentially unchanged and was therefore familiar to everybody.

But in antiquity and in the Middle Ages philosophy and science had fewer points of contact. The philosopher, in erecting his transcendental structure, is himself imbued with the "scientific" world picture of his time and therefore hardly ever makes explicit mention of it. But a philosophical system, since it is in fact a superstructure erected above that concrete concept of the world, must remain incomprehensible to us as long as no precise details are given of its fitting in with the living beliefs then prevailing in special sciences as well as in "experience of life," in tradition, in mythology. Pierre Duhem's study of fourteenth-century physics, which showed how surprisingly near the scholastics had come to modern physics, effected a general revision of the history of scholasticism.

literal etymological sense of something "ultra" or beyond the patent. The one evident thing upon which I can rely is my own life. The transparency or *evidence* of my personal life does not mean freedom from problems, puzzles, mysteries. But my problems as such are clear and unquestionable; that is why they are problems, puzzles, and mysteries. There is an evidence of problems as there is an evidence of solutions, and the second is based on the first. To understand other people, I have nothing else to resort to than the stuff that is my life. Only my life has of itself "meaning" and is therefore intelligible.[8] The situation appears ambiguous, and so it is in a way. With my own life I must understand precisely what it is in alien life that makes it distinct from and strange to mine. My life is the universal interpreter. And history as an intellectual discipline is the systematic endeavor to make of any other human being an *alter ego*, in which expression both terms—the *alter* and the *ego*—must be taken at their full value. Here lies the ambiguity, and this is why the situation presents a problem to reason.

The entire road by which my mind passes from my life to perception of alien life may be epitomized in these four stations:

1. Nothing is present and patent to me except my life. But I do not yet recognize the reality "my life" as mine exclusively. The other human lives that occur within the realm of my life appear interchangeable, as to their contents, with my life. For, having not yet realized the exclusive character of my life which makes it mine and mine solely, I candidly project it into other lives and take it for granted that all people think, feel, and desire what I think, feel, and desire—in short that there is only one undifferentiated form of life in all people.

2. I realize that my neighbor's life is not present and patent to me, but that only symptoms of it reach me. These symptoms show certain abstract characters bearing resemblance to my life, for which reason I presume that behind them lies some-

---

[8] And, vice versa, I am for this reason constantly under the impression that others do not understand me.

thing that also is life. Yet at the same time they display disquieting features which are strange and odd or, which amounts to the same, unintelligible. It is then that the other man strikes me as something uncanny, a creature whom I thought to be like me and who has the effrontery to be different. I discover that life is not always present and patent and intelligible, but that it may be concealed, impenetrable, and other—in one word, that there is alien life. This first particular life to come into view is the *you*, the impact with whose uncanniness makes me conscious of my being nothing but *I*. The *I* is born after the *you* and in reaction upon it, as the rebound from the awful discovery of the *you*, the other as such who has the impudence to be other.

3. Once I have "estranged" my neighbor from myself and he has turned for me into the mystery of the *you*, I take pains to assimilate him. Departing from my life, which now is nothing but *I* and which is the only thing present, patent, and intelligible with which I reckon, I strive to construe my neighbor as an *I* who is another *I*—an *alter ego*, something at once near and distant. This is the point at which begins a great and always problematic enterprise called understanding other people.

4. My neighbor, who had assumed an uncanny aspect, has now come to be partly assimilated or made to resemble me. In fact, of my contemporary—the fellow being with whom I co-exist—I always hope that, in the last instance, he may be like me. Or put differently, my neighbor, though being the *other*, does not seem to be irremediably bound to be *other* than I. I continue to feel that, in principle, he could be I. Love and friendship live on this belief and this hope; they are extreme forms of assimilation between the *I* and the *you*. But people of bygone times are not simply different from me as are my contemporaries; they have no possible way of not being different. That *you* are *you*—that is, that you are not like me—is a mere fact which I cannot help hoping may ultimately be remedied. For that I call you my neighbor (nigh Boor—that is, nigh dweller). But denizens of other times can never dwell so near

me. Their being other than I is not a mere fact, but essentially incurable.[9] And thus an ultimate assimilation is impossible.

Otherwise the past might return and become present again. Another Caesar and another Cleopatra might be born. Past generations are past, not because, in an adventitious chronology, they are located in times that as such are past, but the other way around: the dead cannot come out of the days of yore that are past, and live over again in another time that is present, because their reality is essentially different from the reality of the present and consequently from me. Their being *forever* and *irretrievably* other than I distinguishes them from my mere "neighbor" and gives them a character of inexorable "remoteness" and "ancientness." The vision of the remote as irrevocably remote, the discovery of "ancientness," constitutes the historical perspective which therefore presupposes the realization of the radical otherness of former men. Whereas of my contemporary I always hope that he may at last become like me, I have in my intercourse with ancient man no other way of understanding him than to assimilate myself imaginatively to him—that is, to become that other man. The technique of such intellectual unselfishness is the science of history.

As consciousness of the *you* generates and shapes the consciousness of the *I*, so will awareness of the extreme *you*, ancient man, help present man to acquire supreme consciousness of his exclusive *I*.

"Historical sense" is a sense indeed—a function and an organ to perceive the bygone as such. It is this organ that grants to man the farthest distance he can travel away from himself, while at the same time it presents him, as by rebound, with the clearest understanding an individual can gain of himself. For

---

[9] Those that were, the dead, can no longer change. They are inexorably what they once were. Of a living man we can never definitely say what he is, because he may yet change. It is this immutability of the dead that Mallarmé tries to express when he says in his verse on Edgar Allan Poe's death: *"Tel qu'en lui même l'éternité le change."* The essence of human being is change, and the last change is that which precludes further change, closing the possibilities and fixing "one's self" forever.

when, in his effort to understand former generations, he comes upon the suppositions under which they lived, and that means upon their limitations, he will, by the same token, realize what are the implied conditions under which he lives himself and which circumscribe his existence. By the detour called history he will become aware of his own bounds, and that is the one and only way open to man by which to transcend them.

THERE IS NO HISTORY OF IDEAS PROPER

Before we ventured on this brief digression we pointed out some shortcomings of the current histories of philosophy and, correspondingly, suggested some desiderata. But those random remarks make it clear that history of philosophy stands in need of a thorough reform. The work done during the last fifty years and the ensuing progress are admirable. But for this very reason the discipline has now reached a point of maturity which calls for a fundamental revision.

Letting pass before our inner eye the motion picture of twenty-six centuries of uninterrupted philosophical endeavor, and coming to think of all the anguish, the illusions, efforts, talents, skills, sacrifices, quarrels, enthusiasms, rancors, and ecstasies, all the sinking and rallying of the heart concentrated in the history of the philosophical quest, we cannot help asking with melancholy, particularly in these tense and cruel days which demand close figuring in everything: What good was it all, and what use will it ever be? In such moments it comes home with a shock that our histories of philosophy do not even pose that question. Worse still, they do not even provide the elements necessary for us to ask and answer it for ourselves. After having studied any history of philosophy—and some certainly are voluminous—we are as much in the dark as before about the part philosophy has played in historical reality. And thus we waver preposterously between trusting philosophy to be the major occurrence in any epoch, and hence the guiding power of human destiny throughout these twenty-six centuries, and questioning, in our darker moods, whether philosophy has ever been more than a bee in a bonnet.

In this predicament we cannot help suspecting that what we are accustomed to call history of philosophy is neither "history" nor "of philosophy." Not that I mean to slight the really herculean efforts that have been made in the study of philosophical texts. I admire this work as work; but should this admirable and praiseworthy work really be called history of philosophy? For, what have we been accustomed to understand by this title and this discipline? Simply the exposition of philosophical doctrines in chronological order; or special studies, likewise mere expositions, on those doctrines individually; or studies on one particular thesis or concept in one of them.

Let us briefly analyze: A doctrine is a series of propositions. Propositions are sentences. A sentence is the verbal expression of a "meaning"—what we are accustomed to call idea or thinking. We read or hear the sentence. But what we understand—if we understand it—is its meaning. It is the meaning that is intelligible. Very well; but it is erroneous to believe that a sentence "has its meaning" in an absolute way, apart from when or for whom it was said or written. Nothing is "absolutely intelligible." But the customary histories of philosophy take the opposite for granted. The doctrines are presented to us as though enunciated by the "Unknown Philosopher," an anonymous and abstract being without a birth date or a dwelling place, who is nothing but the author of those writings and therefore does not add anything to their content, neither qualifying nor sharpening it. The date ascribed to a doctrine in such histories of philosophy is no more than an external label tacked on by the historian for his own orientation and for the purpose of establishing some kind of order in the profusion of doctrines. When he tells us that Plato's philosophy is of the fourth century B.C., he means to say that it occurred between 400 and 300 B.C. But he does not realize what his assertion ought to signify, namely, that Plato's philosophy *is* fourth century, that it is made of a peculiar stuff:

the structure of human life in that century; more exactly, in the time of that definite generation.

Or again: when he announces that he is going to present Kant's philosophy, he does not use these words in their full import. He does not propose to understand those doctrines as having been thought and advanced by a man of flesh and bone called Immanuel Kant. He will treat of their meaning in an "absolute" way, independent of time and place. Into the phrase "Kant's philosophy" Kant enters not in the concrete role of the person who did the philosophizing but as an adventitious name connected with a philosophy. Yet the true and real philosophy of Kant is inseparable from the man. This philosophy is one with Kant thinking, pronouncing, writing it; in other words, Kant's philosophy consists in what was actually thought by Kant.

In principle it is always possible to gather *some* sense from the expression of an idea. What is said always conveys *some* signification. But this haphazard meaning is not the authentic meaning of the expression. For language is, by its own nature, equivocal. No saying says of itself all it wants to say. It says a small fraction, and the rest is implied and taken as a matter of course. This defectiveness is congenital to language. If in speaking we had to say all we mean to say so as to preclude ambiguity, language would be impossible. What we actually convey is dependent on innumerable things that remain silent. Language exists through the possibility of reticence, and what is communicated lives on that which is left unsaid and taken for granted. The tacit supplement, which by far outweighs the explicit part in any sentence, is put across in various ways, above all through that which has been said before and that which follows. Every text presents itself as a fragment of a context. Text and context in their turn presuppose, and allude to, a situation out of which has arisen what is actually said. This situation is ultimately inexpressible. It can only be witnessed or imagined. The real situation, out of which the speaking or writing is done, constitutes the integral context of an expression.

Language functions in relation to a situation, implying it and calling for it.

What occurs in the case of words happens to an even higher degree with the idea itself. An idea always is more than its own exclusive appearance. Every idea stands out against a background of other ideas, reference to which is carried within itself. Moreover, an idea by itself and the complex of ideas to which it belongs are themselves not only ideas—that is, pure, abstract "meaning," self-sufficient and self-sustaining. An idea is the reaction of a man upon a definite situation of his life. That is to say, we have grasped the reality of an idea, the idea in its entirety, complete and precise, only if we have taken it as a concrete reaction upon a concrete situation. An idea is inseparable from its corresponding situation. Thinking is a dialogue with circumstance. Of our own situation, like it or no, we are always implicitly conscious. That is why we understand ourselves. But to understand others we must realize what their circumstances are, or it will be as though, listening to a dialogue, we heard the lines of only one of the speakers.

Here we have the first principle of a "new philology." *An idea is an action* taken by a man in view of a definite situation and for a definite purpose. If in endeavoring to comprehend an idea we disregard the circumstances that engendered it and the intention that inspired it, we shall be left with only a vague and abstract outline of the idea. It is precisely this indistinct scheme or skeleton of an idea that is currently called an idea; for it can easily be understood and it has a ubiquitous and "absolute" meaning. But an idea acquires its authentic content and its true and precise "meaning" only in fulfilling the active role for which it was invented and which consists in its functioning with regard to a given situation. Hence there are no "eternal ideas." Each idea is irremediably connected with a situation in which it performs its active role and executes its function.

There are, in point of fact, elements of situations, abstract patterns of circumstances, which occur in more than one individual life. What we call an epoch is a special community effected by homogeneity of circumstance. Ideas conceived in the same epoch have more affinity with each other than with ideas of other epochs. Finally, there are certain ultimate, most abstract patterns of circumstances that may be found in every human life. That is why we are able to gather *some* sort of meaning from any expression and to understand somehow the so-called absolute value of an idea. Even here, however, we understand what we understand—and it is but a blurred fragment of the idea—only because we have recourse to permanent patterns of human situation.

But it is clear that no real situation has ever consisted of such patterns only. Life is concrete, and so are circumstances. Only after having reconstructed the concrete situation and the function of the idea in it can we hope for a true understanding of the idea. But when we take the idea in its abstract sense, which in principle it always holds out to us, the idea will be a dead idea, a mummy, and its content that vague suggestion of human form peculiar to a mummy.

From all this it follows inevitably that the so-called philosophical doctrines have no reality, that they are abstractions. "Doctrines" do not float in air; they are anchored in definite times and places; shorn of their functioning in individual lives, they are ghosts and abstractions. But of abstractions there is no history. History is the form of research that is required for the understanding of the peculiar reality that is human life. Only a living human function, such as it is while it lives—and that means while it functions in the whole of a human existence—allows of history. The Ionic word *historie* signified "information," "ascertainment," and therefore applied indiscriminately to investigation on natural and on human phenomena. But under penalty of having to invent a new word, we must now give to "history" a more exclusive meaning, confining it to the discipline that is concerned with human reality. Human life is the entity that in every moment exists in sight of a past which continues to be alive and active in the present.

These are the two reasons for which I made bold to assert that a "history of philosophy" as chronological exposition of philosophical doctrines is neither "history" nor "of philosophy." It is precisely an abstraction of authentic history of philosophy.

A "history of ideas"—philosophical, mathematical, political, religious, economic—in the traditional sense is impossible. Those ideas, I repeat, which are but abstractions of ideas, have no history.

A conception of doctrines as mere "doctrines" uproots them from their time-environment, with the result that the "philosophies" of twenty-six centuries are offered to us on one and the same plane of time—as of our own day. We seem invited to judge whether Parmenides, Plotinus, or Duns Scotus "are right" in the same way that Bergson, Whitehead, or Husserl are right. Those ancient philosophers are introduced as our contemporaries, heedless of the fact that it is the date that constitutes the essence and the authentic meaning of their writings. Or, which is the same: the statement that Parmenides belongs to the sixth century B.C. should not serve as incidental information, simply to remind us that "naturally in his time people thought that way." No, it is not that Parmenides' ideas may appear more estimable and perhaps pardonable, considering his time, but that, if we fail to see them in relation to their date, we do not understand them well, we simply do not know them—no matter what our final verdict on them may be.

Nor will it do to believe that we have written history when we have shown the influence of an idea upon subsequent ideas. Yesterday's idea does not influence that of today. It influences a man who reacts with a new idea. Any attempt to write history without speaking of men and groups of men is doomed.

To sum up: History must abolish the dehumanized form in which it has offered us the philosophical doctrines. It must incorporate them again in the dynamic interplay of a man's life and let us witness their teleological functioning in it. What if all the inert and mummified ideas which the customary history of philosophy has presented to us arose and functioned again, resuming the part they played in the existence of those who wrestled with them? Would not all those patterns of thought light up with a universal *evidence* to gratify us, their historians who revived them, as they gratified the original thinkers and the students around them?

EVOLUTION OF THE HISTORY OF PHILOSOPHY

History of philosophy begins with Aristotle's reports on earlier solutions to the problems that occupy him. But this is not yet history proper. The solutions are present to his mind as possibilities collaborating with his own efforts. At best he speaks of former philosophers as οἱ ἀρχαῖοι οἱ παλαιοί, the ancients; but the notion "ancient" is not further qualified.[10] Then comes the collector, the eternal initiator of new disciplines. Collections of philosophical opinions are being published—the *placita philosophorum*. After him comes the skeptic, who is concerned to point out the dissonance of opinions—διαφονία τῶν δοξῶν—as a proof that truth is not to be had. Thus Sextus Empiricus is one of the ancient authors who furnishes us with most details on earlier philosophers. This manner of writing history of philosophy continues with variations through many centuries, till the tradition is legitimized by the eighteenth century, which holds it to be the mission of history of philosophy to unfold the panorama of human folly. History becomes the account of *human errors, of* intellectual discrepancies. The variety of opinions advanced by mankind in the course of time appears essentially negative in view of the "one and lasting truth" attained by that blessed century. It would be hard to imagine a flatter denial of historical reality in our sense than is implied in that sort of "history." As late as 1742 Bruckner announces that he is going to pass in review the *"infinita falsae philosophiae exempla."*

Kant's profound revision of philosophy, requiring a restatement of all problems from the very bottom, sets the philosopher —as in the pristine hour of Aristotle—to looking for the collabo-

[10] In *Physics* I, 8, 191b, 34, he calls them ignorant, ὑπ' ἀπειρίας.

ration of the past. Again the needs of the workshop bring the philosopher into touch with earlier doctrines. But this time the movement coincides with the development of the "historical sense" and the new techniques it engendered: philology, criticism of sources, time-perspective.

However, we have today not yet passed much beyond the point of view of the workshop. And that prevents us from fully accomplishing such historical study of philosophy as searches for the integral reality of past philosophy and not only for the abridgment that present-day philosophers need as a manual for their private alchemy. But a slight infiltration of "historical sense" into the history of philosophy has sufficed to bring about important rearrangements in the picture of former thought. What looked like a smothering maze of errors and clashing opinions—and thus like something completely irrational—begins to appear as an ordered evolution, a continuity in which human thinking progresses rationally from one conception to another. The systems succeed each other in intelligible descent. And a residue of irreducible discrepancy between a variety— a fixed variety—of points of view loses the character of arbitrariness. The impossibility of comprehending the universe of the real in its entirety from *one* point of view gives a clear meaning to the existence of a variety of fundamental conceptions, which thus proves to be inevitable.[11] In the irrational chaos of man's philosophical past, the contour of "historical reason" begins to be discernible.

PHILOSOPHY AND SOCIETY

Philosophy is not only a function in the philosopher's own life, but also a doctrine he brings before the public. The public is more than such or such individual persons. It is a community of

[11] Cf. Wilhelm Dilthey, "Typen der Weltanschauung und ihre Ausbildung in den metaphysischen Systemen," in *Gesammelte Schriften*, B. G. Teubner, 1922–1931, vol. VII, p. 75.

men, a society. We thus find that philosophy is also a function in collective life, a social fact, an institution. And all these forms of existence are included in the reality "philosophy."

For those to whom the foregoing has not seemed entirely cogent, it will at this point become obvious that a history of philosophy cannot consist simply in a chronological exposition of "doctrines" or, which is the same, that the reality "philosophy" cannot be reduced to "ideas."

In fact, if we wish to answer in due order the question: What is philosophy? we must begin with describing how and where we first find philosophy, its immediate aspect—"the first for us," as Aristotle would say. Now, before philosophy means anything to the inner life of present-day man he comes upon it as a public reality which even possesses material attributes. There are buildings connected with it and jobs that enable a man to make a living; he also sees it in the guise of books, produced by an industry and sold commercially. Proof that this is the primary aspect of philosophy may be found in the fact that these things are known to people who know least about philosophy. The true philosopher, who lives steeped in meditation upon the innermost problems of philosophy, may tend to disregard this first aspect. But he is ill advised when he makes a principle of such disregard. For it is clear that all these attributes form no negligible part of the integral reality of "philosophy." If the state endows and maintains professorships of philosophy, if publishers are anxious to issue philosophical books, there obviously operates in society a valid belief that philosophy is a collective need. And that is much. And it would be a mistake to overlook it merely because it is obvious. Why, how, and to what degree is philosophy a collective need? What modifications, what ups and downs has the belief that it is a collective need suffered in the history of societies from the beginning of philosophy in Greece? History of philosophy has done little to answer these questions. That is why we philosophers, as I have said before, find ourselves in the preposterous predicament of having no certainty as to the "importance" in history of our discipline and our occupation.

And the fact is that the reality of all things human consists precisely in their "importance." Any manifestation of my life, however insignificant, refers to my existence as a whole and can reveal its true value and meaning only when conceived in relation to my whole life. What I do and what happens to me have reality only in so far as they import me. In humanities, therefore, rather than of "things" (a concept taken from the sciences and good there for provisional use only) we should speak of "importances." But incredible though it seems, no book proposes to tell us the story of the "importance" of philosophy from the beginnings to our day; or even in any definite epoch. Only here and there may an author briefly and obliquely glance at this immense complex of problems.[12]

Here we have philosophy *functioning* in social life, as an item in state budgets, as a requirement officially imposed upon generation after generation of students. When things exist by reason of the state, and public power takes them into its hands, they are not a social reality simply and plainly, they are so superlatively; for the state is the superlative of society. The state does not take up a matter if society has not felt it to be an indispensable need. For thousands of years no philosophy existed, and for hundreds of years man philosophized but the state did not care. Then came a day when the state began its dealings with philosophy—avoiding it and pursuing it. Came another day, and philosophy was made a normal public institution. What Plato postulated as a utopian ideal whose realization would have frightened Plato himself became in time a fact. How far Plato was from believing that philosophy could ever acquire social functions is revealed in the *Apology*. When Socrates pleads before his judges that his endeavors to inveigle people into meditation should be considered not criminal but

[12] The only period investigated to some extent from this point of view is the eighteenth century in France, the time of the *philosophes*.

a public service entitling him to eat in the Prytaneum at the cost of the state, his declaration is set down as an amusing paradox and a piece of consummate irony.

Philosophy has not only "official" reality as an institution, and economic reality as a commodity brought into the market by the publishing industry; it has reality of yet another form in public opinion. For centuries on end, the philosopher has enjoyed prestige, and prestige is a social agency. Here we come upon another subject for future histories of philosophy: the waxing and waning of the prestige of the philosopher. Few studies are likely to yield deeper insight into human history than a reconstruction of the social lot suffered and enjoyed by the philosopher, a precise account of the position accorded by different periods and different societies to the professor of philosophy.

At this point we are thrown back as by rebound from philosophy as a social reality to the manner in which philosophy affects the philosopher; for, as I have indicated, the social position in which he finds himself has not a little to do with the part his ideas play in his own life. He thinks not only at a precise time and in a definite place, he also thinks from a social station which sometimes lies in the center of society, sometimes below, sometimes above it, and which may happen to be outside society: in prison or exile. It would be of great interest to determine for each period the exact dose of freedom allowed to the philosopher. What were the effects of lack of freedom? But let us not fail to ask the opposite question, too: How did philosophy react upon an overdose of freedom? An entire book might be written under the title: On the Responsibility and Irresponsibility of Philosophy.[13] And analogous questions must be asked as to the

[13] I have partially finished an essay in which I treat of this subject, intertwining it, however, with another more general theme: Discourse on Intellectual Responsibility. In it I refer, as to an example and a guiding principle, to the evolution of French thought. For of all Western civilizations that of France has suffered least from interruptions, from the Renaissance to our day. The situation in France during the war prevented me, for the time being, from finishing my study.

effects of praise and of neglect. I do not know that I should call
the first beneficent and the second pernicious.

The first aspect presented by the reality "philosophy" derives,
we have said, from what it is as a social fact. In the great external
world of public phenomena we meet the institution of philosophy as we meet politics, boards of health, the fire brigade, the
executioner, national holidays, or fashions. For a long time now
society has obviously needed to have a certain number of its
members imbued with philosophical opinions, as it has for
about a century needed to have them vaccinated.

The social constituent of philosophy clearly forms the most
superficial part of its reality—the bark of the tree, as it were.
Society is never original and creative. For society to be concerned with philosophy, philosophy must first exist, and its
creation depends on a few individuals.

AUTHENTICITY AND UNAUTHENTICITY
OF PHILOSOPHY

It behooves us to understand very clearly the way in which
philosophy—and not only philosophy—is forever journeying
back and forth between the public and the individual. A person
first finds philosophy in his surroundings as a public usage and
an institution independent of any *definite* individual. Even if
for the time being no authentic philosopher and, consequently,
no authentic philosophy exist, philosophy endures as a social
reality. Professors of philosophy will go on teaching; books of
alleged philosophy will continue to be sold; and so on. For it is
characteristic of social agents (usages, customs, laws, etc.) that
they exist and function independently of any *definite* individual. We must keep in mind that a social act is done simply because "it is done." The anonymous pressure of the collective
body around us compels us—by physical or moral compulsion
—to act in a certain way. There is no link between our doing

and the reason *why* we are doing it. The professor of philosophy
may happen to be no philosopher at all; he teaches philosophy
in order to make a living or to be socially distinguished. The
student takes philosophy because he has to. The social reality
a phenomenon has acquired—its validity—does not in the least
guarantee its human genuineness. Social reality implies no authenticity whatever. Or, which is the same, all social reality is
unauthentic.

It is precisely its unauthenticity that enables a social agent
to fulfill its collective purpose of holding sway for individuals,
with or without the explicit adherence of any definite person—
in short, mechanically. If a social function ultimately depended
on definite individuals, it would, as these can and in fact sometimes do fail it, easily vanish away. But a society maintains its
binding beliefs—in philosophy, for instance—with a blindness
not altogether harmful; it maintains them irrationally, in the
same way that nature sticks to her lines of conduct. This makes
it clear that society's need of philosophy and consequently the
reality of philosophy as a social fact are an unauthentic need
and an unauthentic reality.

After this brief elucidation of a difficult point let us now return to what I have called the journeying back and forth of philosophy. We said that the individual first finds philosophy un-
related to any definite person in impersonal society. But society
as such would not be concerned with philosophy, and support
it mechanically, if it had not found philosophy ready-made in
certain individuals. Those individuals are the makers of philosophy. And they made philosophy because they felt, each for himself, the need of it. This need felt by the creative individual is
the authentic and original need. In him and not in society lies
the *origin* and the authentic or fundamental reality of philosophy.[14]

---

[14] Nature does not admit of degrees of reality. Things exist or do not exist,
and that is all. To possess varying degrees of reality is characteristic of human
phenomena. What man does can be more or less authentic and hence more or
less real. But unauthentic reality of something—be it philosophy, be it a man's
"goodness"—is not simply identical with unreality. It has its own reality, the

This perpetual swinging to and fro of all human matters, from the individual to the collective and back again to the individual, is a general condition of our existence, entailing, like all things human, at once conveniences and inconveniences. When human dealings establish themselves as social facts, they become mechanical and unauthentic—ideas grow hackneyed—but thanks to such transformation they are also freed from the

reality peculiar to the unauthentic. To give a formal wording to this thesis, we may say that any human reality possesses a scale of defective modes against one "plenary mode" which is its "authenticity." All these modes together constitute the integral reality of the respective human phenomenon. Anything social is intrinsically and not by chance a human phenomenon in its unauthentic form; and social existence is a defective—albeit inevitable—mode of being-a-man which belongs to every personality.

Plato points out this difference between the authentic and the unauthentic in human ways. And he does so, sure enough, when speaking of philosophy and the state (public offices). In the *Republic* VII, 535, he says: "The mistake at present is that those who study philosophy have no vocation, and this, as I was saying before, is the reason why she has fallen into disrepute; her true sons should take her by the hand and not bastards." Here authenticity and unauthenticity of the philosophical pursuit appear with the names of "bastard" and "true son." A few lines below, when speaking of the virtues of men and of rulers in particular—that is, of political activity and of public offices—Plato adds ". . . should we not carefully distinguish between the true son and the bastard?" Further proof that Plato was aware of these two modes of human reality is given by the fact that in a paragraph between the two passages quoted, he speaks of "involuntary falsehood" into which man may blunder, and contrasts it with voluntary and deliberate falsehood, *pseudos akusion.* We could not find a better word for what we have here called unauthenticity. Man always stands in danger of being but a pseudo self.

About social phenomena and the execution of official functions we shall hear Plato say: "Without realizing it we allow public services to be performed haphazardly by people who lack the virtues required for such occupation." Plato does not here employ the term virtue which I introduce. But the word is implied in the whole paragraph. For the Greek, virtue—*areté*—means nothing else than authenticity—that is, "actual capability" or simply "capability" of something; being what one is in full reality. Everything living possesses its *areté,* its virtue, namely its *plenary mode* of being.

Plato speaks very frequently of what has "more being" and what has "less being" (cf. the *Republic* IX, 586; VII, 515). This has nothing to do with the argument with which in *Phaidon* Plato refutes the definition of the soul as harmony by saying that, as some souls are more harmonious than others, this definition would imply that a soul may have more or less being—which is impossible. Neither does Aristotle admit that substances can have degrees of being. It is clear that Aristotle's substances, like Plato's ideas, possess supreme being, and that supreme being does not allow of gradation. Aristotle admits "more or less being" in the other categories. Let us not forget that for Aristotle the being of substance is not just any being but the "principal being," κυρίως ὅν.

whims, the frailty, and the arbitrariness of individuals. In the following we shall be concerned with an inconvenience that proves to be particularly grave in the case of philosophy.

HISTORY OF PHILOSOPHY AS REGRESS

For many centuries it has now been the case that an individual, before himself having felt an urge to philosophize, encounters philosophy as a publicly established and maintained occupation, which means that he is invited to occupy himself with philosophy for unauthentic reasons: for the security and social prestige it offers as a profession; or—a "purer" but not less unauthentic motive—from curiosity or enthusiasm. That all these motives are unauthentic, if unauthentic to a varying degree, is shown by the fact that they all presuppose an already existing philosophy. The professional philosopher learns and teaches ready-made doctrines. The enthusiast beholds the completed systems and is delighted by their accomplished form; and so on. But this is most pernicious, for thus we risk becoming immersed in an occupation whose inner meaning we have had neither time nor opportunity to discover. The same happens with almost all human occupations. Since they "are there," we may choose an occupation mechanically and devote our whole life to it without ever coming into touch with its essential reality.

Whereas the true philosopher, who is a philosopher because he cannot help being one, has little use for existing philosophy. He begins by making his own. Indeed, to be dissatisfied with, and in opposition to, all previous philosophical thought, and to withdraw into the fearful solitude of his own meditation, is the infallible sign of a born philosopher.

Undramatic though it appears, the constant invitation to unauthenticity that arises from the social pre-existence of human occupations forms one of the tragic elements of human life. Hence the necessity of combining apprenticeship in philosophy and study of socially established and recommended doctrines with the determination to question them all and to *begin afresh* or, which is the same, to restore the primordial situation in which philosophy was born. Those first philosophers who absolutely made philosophy because it was absolutely nonexistent —or, strictly speaking, got it under way, for they did not yet succeed in making it—are the true professors of philosophy to whom we must hark back across all the din set up by all subsequent professors of philosophy.

Any great philosopher has been great because he reproduced in his person, at least approximately, that pristine situation. For this reason it is of great importance to commune also with those great renewers of the philosophical quest. But alas, traditional history of philosophy hardly promotes such intercourse with the great philosophers of the past. Since it does nothing to evoke the individual drama of their existence, it fails to revive the essential spectacle of their philosophies arising from that drama.

History of philosophy is a subdiscipline of philosophy and not an annex to satisfy impertinent curiosity. For two reasons: First, a philosopher, in working out his system, always stands within definite traditions of thinking which surround him so tightly that they seem to be reality itself and are not recognized as merely particular tendencies and essays of the human mind. In order to come into full possession of these traditions, which are, as it were, our intellectual groundwork, we must know them well, down to their most elusive implications, and must state explicitly their most "evident" suppositions. Second, the limitation and bondage resulting from the inexorable necessity of thinking within a definite tradition can be somehow counteracted only by resuscitating philosophy as it was at its origin *when no tradition yet existed*, or in those decisive moments of its later history when it was reborn and, in pursuing partly new aims, retrieved its pristine vigor.

What we said of all human occupations holds good for philosophy. We are in constant danger of swallowing the standard problems hook, line, and sinker, and of performing mechanically, from mere inertia, the established modes of thinking.

And that is fatal. Not because it prevents us from being "original." The hankering after "originality" is a stupid itch. No, the damage to be expected from such an attitude is that in playing the game and accepting the customary ways of thinking and the current manner of putting the problems, we have not even truly grasped the problems. For to "acquire a problem" we must undo it. We must retrace the whole path by which its discoverers advanced when they first came upon it. They started from a philosophical naught—from the pure need of philosophy— without even knowing if and how such a thing could be contrived. Let us quote Goethe: "Whate'er you have, bequeathed you by your father, earn it in order to possess it."

In order to acquire existing philosophy we must begin by breaking it up till we come to its very core where it is nothing but need and vexing absence of philosophy. There is no other way of remaking a philosophy—nor philosophy in general— than by taking it to pieces, as one knows an engine only after having dismantled it. The ever lengthening history of philosophical thought behind us and the ever growing wealth of concepts, methods, and theories garnered make it all the more urgent to return to the primordial poverty and that radical need of philosophy from which its later profusion has sprung.

This intrepid regress toward the origins, in the process of which we break up all the philosophical systems in order to witness again their exemplary birth, constitutes the substance of the history of philosophy.

For we cannot be authentically occupied with philosophy without knowing what philosophy is. The question splits in two. What has philosophy been? What is it going to be? History of philosophy takes it upon itself to answer the first question by retracing the long journey of intellectual evolution back to the sixth century B.C., to that extraordinary hour when something that had not existed before suddenly came into being: philosophy.

The historical circumstances of so extraordinary a period cannot fail to be of extraordinary interest. But here again history of philosophy forsakes us. No thorough investigation informs us of what happened then, why at that moment and in Greece Western man began to philosophize.

PHILOSOPHY IS A TRADITION

In saying that philosophical inquiry is carried on within a definite tradition of thinking, I have not said everything. Not only does my particular philosophy emerge from a particular intellectual tradition—of a people, of an epoch, of a school—but philosophy as a whole is one immense tradition. The philosopher is apt to labor under the delusion that the opposite holds, for it is true that essentially philosophy consists in the attempt to exist without tradition. Tradition is a peculiar form of sleep-walking. It makes a man think, feel, desire in forms that from time out of mind have prevailed in his human environment and about whose validity he feels no misgivings whatever. The system of traditions supersedes in man the system of instincts which as an animal he has lost. In so far as I live submerged in a tradition, I obey it instinctively and thus lead a life of pure "faith," the life of a true "believer."

But the truth is that philosophy in its turn is nothing if not the tradition of nontradition; so much so that the best definition of philosophy—and one richer in content than first appears, for at first it seems to say almost nothing—would be of a chronological character: philosophy is an intellectual occupation that Western man has felt urged to exercise since the sixth century B.C. and that, with strange constancy, he has been exercising ever since.

In order that philosophy be born, life in the form of pure tradition must have become impossible; man must have lost "the faith of his forebears." Then the individual person remains isolated and uprooted, and nothing but his own exertion will help him to find new ground on which to settle in new security. Only where this happens and to the extent to which it happens have we philosophy.[15] Philosophy is not a caprice or a pastime; it is one of man's reactions to the irremediable fact that some day "the faithful" fall into doubt. It is the movement of a swimmer striving to keep afloat on the "sea of doubts." Or in another image, it is the treatment man applies to the dreadful wound which his faith in breaking off has torn open in his innermost being.

As tradition takes the place of failing instinct, so philosophy is a substitute for shattered tradition. All man's doings are substitutes, and each substitute preserves fastened on its back the corpse of what it has been called upon to replace. Thus philosophy *seems* to go against "tradition" and against "faith." But in truth it is not that philosophy killed tradition and faith, but that tradition and faith sickened and died, and philosophy had to take up the mantle as best she could. Owing to an optical distortion peculiar to human affairs, succession looks like ejection and assassination, while in reality the apparent enemy is bent on prolonging the virtue of the dead, and to that end slips into the vacant place.

Loss of faith does not necessarily engender philosophy. Man may find no way of keeping afloat in the sea of doubts into which he has fallen, indeed may go down to the very bottom. The bottom means despair. There are whole "civilizations of despair" made up by the measures man takes when despair becomes a permanent attitude.[16] An example of such a civilization of despair is provided by the "sapiental literature" (Assyrian, Egyptian, Greek, Hebrew) which, oddly and disconcertingly enough, is the *oldest literature extant*. Nothing worth mentioning has been said about it. I hope to treat of it soon with some thoroughness.

[15] The Middle Ages produced philosophy in proportion as faith weakened.

[16] Despair always appears qualified by the special things man is despairing of. When a "faith" dies the ensuing form of despair tends to lead to one or another form of knowledge. But there also exists "despair of knowledge" which may inaugurate a new epoch of faith. Cicero expresses in a highly paradoxical manner his state of mind and that of his contemporaries, the Academics, saying—*De finibus* II, XIV—that they were *quasi desperata cognitione certi*—certain of the all but desperate situation of knowledge. It was through the breach of this despair that Christianity made its entrance into history.

Philosophy, if born of despair, does not remain in it. The philosopher believes he has found a passage through the frightful straits, and he calls it a "way"—*hodos, methodos* [17]—a word that again and again appears in the early philosophers (Parmenides, Heraclitus). This indicates that *philosophy is a belief, too,* the belief that man possesses a faculty called reason which enables him to discover the true reality and to establish himself in it.

This faith sets going the peculiar tradition that is philosophy [18]—that mixture of perspicacity and blindness. The faith is alive in us. There always remains in man a last dose of somnambulism left over from the animal he once was.

HISTORY OF PHILOSOPHY AS PROGRESS

History of philosophy, we have seen, begins with the philosopher's *regress* to the *origin* of philosophical tradition—as though the arrow while it flies, cleaving the air, should for a

---

[17] Nobody seems to have noticed how revealing the term *aporia*—question—is for the mood in which the first and decisive steps of philosophy were taken. *Poros* means passage, whence its secondary meanings: way, ford, bridge, straits. But *poros* is not just any passage. It is the passage we discover unexpectedly after having despaired of finding one. Hence *poros* also means recourse, device, expedient, and, consequently, solution; whereas a situation that gives no way out is described by the word *a-poria*, which was used for problem, question, difficulty; in short, for that which looks opaque to the mind and does not allow comprehension to pass through. The word *poros* which rendered the meaning of way with all its inherent drama—a passage needed, seemingly lacking, and suddenly found—was later supplanted by the more tranquil expression *hodos*, the way that is there, ready to be trodden, having been no problem or *a-poria*. For this very reason, however, the new term was soon found unsatisfactory, and the inert conception of a beaten track was intensified by injecting the dynamic meaning of a "going beyond," a step forward on the route, and the certainty of advance. *Hodos* gave way to *met-hodos* which in this case may best be translated by progress. Thus in the word *methodos* the essence of the old meaning of *poros* is revived. *Poros* is connected with the Latin *por-ta* and *por-tus*, which denote an "entrance" on land, by sea, or into a river (cf. V. Meillet, *Linguistique* I, 243). In the Odyssey XII, v. 259, Ulysses speaks of all he suffered when he was looking for the "passages of the sea." A stronger philologist than I would, I am sure, draw a few more sparks from this lexicographic flint.

[18] Cf. p. 68.

moment turn and look back to the bow and the hand that sent
it forth. But such regress has nothing to do with nostalgia or
with the wish to remain in that pristine hour. As he travels back
into the past the philosopher is from the very first inspired by
the purpose of returning to the present, to himself and his own
most actual thinking. Because he knows beforehand that all
past philosophy revolves about his own thought, he cannot
be content with looking down the avenue of philosophical
systems like a tourist doing the sights of a city. He must see
those doctrines from within, and this he can do only by starting
out from the need from which they sprang. So he plunges into
the origin of philosophy in order to return, through the innermost arcana and along the subterranean roads of the philosophical evolution, back to the present day.

In this way each philosophical system becomes lucid and appears as the *necessary* outcome of the human situation that engendered it, but each system also reveals its specific shortcom-
ing from which its successor will take off. The new doctrine is
not simply *another* doctrine; it is in a way the preceding doctrine, too. For the new preserves the old, at least in the mode
of reckoning with it, being conscious of it, and avoiding its
shortcomings and errors. Thus philosophy advances through
time toward the present, accumulating past and integrating
it in each new discovery. The history of philosophy itself discovers that it is *progress* and not merely change and succession.[19]

Up to the eighteenth century, history of philosophy, as we
have said before, was not written in the form of a history of progressing thought. Rather the past was presented as a collection
of errors over and against which the historian's own philosophy
stood out as the truth. This truth did not lie preformed or em-

[19] The accumulation that constitutes the progress of philosophy differs from
that which takes place in the progress of special sciences. In physics we now
know *more* than we did ten centuries ago. Here accumulation has the aspect of
an accretion. In philosophy we know the same today as yesterday. But we know
it with a knowledge of finer grain. Such accumulation is a sort of inner growth.

bryonic in earlier thought. It was something totally new, sprung from the mind in full panoply. It was the contrary of *error*.

The idea of history as progress was first conceived, it is true, in the eighteenth century—by Turgot, Condorcet, Ferguson. But though it had appeared, the conception could not yet establish itself in its true form, pending the development of the "historical sense."

The assumption, which still obtains today, was that one ought to speak of progress in history only if it is possible to point out an absolute "frame of reference" in which to measure the movements of the past. In history of philosophy one should, accordingly, not speak of an effective and demonstrable progress unless there exists a final philosophy whose genesis is discernible in the past. Only in proportion as former thinkers were discovering little by little the elements integrating this definitive philosophy can their doctrines be held to form steps toward a goal— that is, to mark a progress. No doubt, such a progress, which confers in retroaction the value of absolute truth (of non-error) upon earlier doctrines, must be called absolute. But a progress need not be absolute in order to be "absolutely," that is, effectively, progress.

When a philosopher returns from the *origins* of philosophical thinking to his own philosophy, he discovers that all the systems of the past persist in his own thought. If one of them were missing, he would have to revise his opinions in order to take into account the missing one. Philosophy is made in such a way that its present always sees its past come wandering up to it, progressing toward it.[20]

And such a progress is not a hypothesis or an *ad hoc* con-

---

[20] That this progress was recognized only a century and a half ago is to be explained by the fact that up to that time earlier doctrines were looked upon not as past but as *actual* philosophy, differing from the true philosophy and therefore totally erroneous. But even times still blind to the historical perspective were oddly conscious of the collaboration of the past with the present—that is, of progress. What from the late seventeenth century on used to be called eclecticism is but a nonhistorical form of accepting the past and giving credit to its true insights,

struction. It is evidenced to the philosopher in his contact with
the achievements of the intellectual past, providing he has
learned to understand them according to the norms here suggested. This is no doubt a progress relative to his own philosophy, but it is evidently and unquestionably a progress. To be
sure, this phenomenon of evident progression does not imply
that a definitive value is ascribed to his philosophy. But such definitive value would add nothing to the character of progress inherent in the evolution of philosophy. The one thing it would
add is that it lends an absolute character to that evolution and
therefore to the progress of philosophy.

THINKING AND "PROGRESS TOWARD ITSELF"
IN ARISTOTLE

In Aristotle's treatise *On the Soul,* I find a passage of supreme
wisdom which, as far as I know,[21] has never been properly interpreted.

Aristotle's philosophy is a frontal attack on a problem that
had baffled all previous efforts of Greek thinkers: the problem
of "motion" in its most general sense—that of change or trans-
mutation. The prephilosophical and hence fundamental idea
that the Greeks connect with the concept of being is that of
imperturbable rest. Being means identity of a thing with itself;
to be what it is from the beginning and forever; absolute ontological repose. In short, their primal conception of being is
static. We do not propose to venture upon an explanation of
this Hellenic partiality, which is almost an instinct, for the im-
mobility of being. History of philosophy might have troubled
to throw some light on it. But reality is not composed exclusively of things that are changeless and motionless like geo-

---

[21] I cannot be sure about this. As it happens, I am writing without a library
in reach. All I have on hand is Aristotle's text and a tome of old Zeller's, who
does not even touch the subject. It may not be out of place to remind future
readers of the conditions, material and moral, under which we write in these
days—we that still write seriously.

metrical figures. Precisely those phenomena that are nearest to us—natural phenomena—are changeable and in motion. How, then, shall we conceive of being that consists in change and movement?

We come upon change or "movement" in the form of transition. A thing from being something determinate passes into being something else determinate. The thing that is white becomes black. Whiteness and blackness are static being. But the transition in which there is no more whiteness and not yet blackness is a "being on the march" [22] from whiteness to blackness. A being which as being is on the march, at each moment leaves off being what it was and comes to be what it was not, the other. If the thing that is now *actually* white were only white and in no sense black, it could not *change* into black. Or else it must annihilate itself completely, and in that case there would not have occurred a change of color, but the white thing would have been succeeded—if it is permissible in such a case to speak of succession—by the black thing, an entirely new object without any relation to the white one. We should have one entity and another entity, but no transition from the one to the other. Only when we suppose that the thing now actually white is now also potentially black does there appear a gleam of hope that we may comprehend the idea of change.

Not that white turns black, which would be an unintelligible relation, but that the latent blackness in the white thing is set free, as it were, to exist actually and effectively. Thus change means that something a thing has potentially been passes into full or perfect being (*entelecheia*) or into "actual" or operative being (*energeia*). Potential being, while strictly such, has no effectiveness or actuality whatever. It is the opposite of effective or actual being—*Metaphysics* IX, 1048a, 31. It remains hidden and has a repressed reality which is in no way manifest. Now let us imagine that the capability of the white thing of

[22] I do not use the expression "on the march" arbitrarily. The word is apt to slip, under varying guises, from Aristotle's own pen. Thus *Physics* VIII, 5.257b, 7: "the potential marches, βαδίζης, to the entelechy." Or *On the Heavens* IV, 3:311a, 14: "the potential is going, ιὸν, to the entelechy."

being black manifests itself, that the capability becomes effective as such. We then have not yet the black thing, the *actual being black,* but the thing *actually* blackening. Blackening is not yet being black, it is the passage to being black and the change itself. Thus the reality "change" presents itself as the strange way of being that combines the two opposite characters of potentiality and effectiveness. It is potentiality in action or in actuality. On other occasions—for instance, *On the Soul* 417a, 16—Aristotle says that "motion is thought to be a sort of actuality but incomplete, ἀτελής"—that is, a reality that begins to exist with complete being but does not end so.

When he has reached this point Aristotle may be seen passing his hand across his brow as, with a weary sigh, he informs us, *Physics* 201b, 33: "Indeed, it is hard to grasp what motion is." But all other attempts at a solution having failed, "there remains, then, the suggested mode of definition, namely, that it is a sort of actuality, or actuality of the kind described, hard to grasp, but not incapable of existing."

After this definition Aristotle feels satisfied regarding the ontological nature of change. But his subtle mind cannot help noticing that there are two major classes of change—which incidentally reveals that under the dialectical formalism peculiar to his thinking his immediate intuition of the phenomena as they present themselves remains keenly alert.[23]

The change of something white into something black begins in the white thing and *ends* in its being black. Every change, being passage and transition, has a *terminus a quo* and a *terminus ad quem.* The word *terminus*—πέρας—expresses very well that when arriving at it the change terminates.[24] In our example the end of the change is "being black," and being black is a reality distinct from blackening; the changing is different from

---

[23] For Aristotle's clear awareness of his own intellectual behavior cf. *On Generation and Corruption* I, 316a, 5, where he declares that "those whom devotion to abstract discussions has rendered unobservant of the facts are too ready to dogmatize on the basis of a few observations."

[24] In *Metaphysics* 1048b, 18, which is the decisive passage, πέρας is opposed to τέλος, and we must decide which to translate by "end" and which by *terminus* or "limit."

its end or, which is the same, the end is not present in the change proper. The other examples cited by Aristotle are of the same type. Reducing is different from being thin; learning from having learned; getting well from being well.

But there exists another reality: man thinking, meditating, "theorizing." Thinking is a change in the person. From being one who does not think of A he passes into one who does think of A. And it is precisely this passage that is thinking. His *coming to think of A* is already a *thinking of A* and continuing to think A while the thinking lasts. On the other hand his *not thinking A* must be understood as *not actually thinking A* but being capable of so doing. Like any other movement, thinking is the release of a potentiality. But here the change is not distinct from its end as becoming black is from being black. The change called thinking contains its *terminus ad quem;* the end is immanent in the movement. In other words the change is performed not for the sake of an entity alien to it but for the sake of the change itself. Let us try to express this in another form. Every movement is a making or a being made of something—namely, the end. In constructing we construct the work—ἔργον. The constructing is the making; the work corresponds to what is made; and when the making arrives at the work the making stops while the product remains. Let us now imagine that the intended product is itself a making, as though we were proposing to go not somewhere but for a walk. Thinking, like all change, is a transition, but with the paradoxical qualification that thinking is not a transition to something else but a marching, advancing, "progressing toward the same"—εἰς αὐτὸ γὰρ ἡ ἐπίδοσις.[25]

Those changes whose end lies beyond the change proper, and which terminate when they reach it, making room for a new stable state and a new actuality or complete being, Aristotle calls movements *sensu stricto*. The above-mentioned examples belong to this class.[26] But a change that terminates in itself, and

[25] This, then, is the passage mentioned above—*On the Soul* II, 5, 417b, 5. We possess a variant that reads "toward itself." However, the discrepancy between the two texts is unimportant, for both readings lead to the same result.

[26] *Metaphysics* IX, 1048b, 33.

that, though being transition and passage and march, marches only to march and not to get somewhere, is what Aristotle calls *action* (*energeia*), being in the fullness of its meaning.[27]

Here we see Aristotle transcend the static idea of being, since not only motion proper but being itself, which seemed to be immutable, reveals itself as action and therefore as a motion *sui generis.*

For a Greek to conceive of being as pure mobility means a tremendous effort. No wonder that at this climax of his philosophical conception Aristotle seems to stagger under the impact of his own discovery. Already when defining "transition toward the other" or motion proper, we saw him shading his eyes as though dazzled by too sudden a light. Now he is worried by scruples which he seeks to shirk. The entire paragraph of the treatise *On the Soul* from which I am quoting trembles with indecision.[28] "It seems not appropriate to give the name of change—alteration—to meditation. Or one should perhaps distinguish between two kinds of change." Indeed, thinking is not only a movement; it is also the end toward which the movement tends, a movement that has from the outset arrived at its end, and that in spite or rather because of that never "ends" but always reissues from itself.

Had Aristotle further examined into the problem which he discovered and which terrified him, he would have come upon this immediate consequence: that the change "thinking," which he contrasts with "change toward the other" (alteration, locomotion, etc.) or motion proper, requires a definition that like-

[27] For movement as limit and end cf. *Metaphysics* 1050a, 17. For the making and the work *ibid.* 21–22. Our word "end" has the double meaning of the thing intended by the movement and the movement coming to a close once its aim is attained. The customary translation of the Aristotelian term *telos* by "end" is appropriate in the case of motion proper, in which the intended end coincides with the conclusion of the movement. But in the case of "action" a distinction must be made between end and limit. An action has τέλος but no πέρας. It has ends but no end.

[28] This paragraph from *On the Soul* must be considered in conjunction with the sixth chapter of the ninth book of *Metaphysics,* the most important part of which—1048b, 18 to 1049a, 34—was unknown in the time of St. Thomas Aquinas.

wise stands in contrast to the definition he gives for motion proper. Hence when he says that "motion" is potentiality in the form of actuality, thinking ought to be described as action being converted into potentiality, as actuality in the form of potentiality. I shall explain myself.

If thinking is movement not toward something else but toward itself, and if it has therefore from the outset reached the intended end, this end being the very thinking, we come to the result that the process of thinking consists in an incessant renewal of the same movement. To understand this as clearly as possible, let us break up the "thinking of A" into a continuous series of "acts" in which A is thought. In such a series the "second" act reactualizes the "first" which had turned into potentiality of the second; and so on. The thing that perplexes Aristotle is that the passage of the initial potentiality into the act of thinking does not entail *extinction of the potentiality but is rather a conservation of what existed potentially by that which exists plenarily (entelechy) so that potentiality and action become like.*[29]

The mode of being that is particular to the phenomenon "thinking" thus consists in a continuous beginning anew of the movement, because the movement has from the outset reached its end, the end being the very potentiality that has been released. Potentiality which immediately becomes effective is continuously reborn as potentiality which then reiterates its actualization. That is the reason why the kind of movement that is

[29] *On the Soul* 417b, 3. The translation is problematic because Aristotle's own mind hesitates before his sublime paradox. May it be noted that of bodily movements the one nearest to the thinking type as I interpret it would be the revolution of the heavens. A more complete study of this whole matter would lead to the problem how to conceive of the "pure act" that is God. But it seems to me that the preliminary step for tackling such a tremendous subject is a precise account of the role that "potentiality" plays in the cismundane "act." And this is what I have been trying, if very briefly, to do here. The basic text for my thesis is the already quoted 417b, 3, which says that in this type of movement "the entelechy saves or preserves—σωτερία—the potentiality." What else can that mean than that action is its own potentiality? For a final elucidation of the question we should have to start from the idea of time. The relation "before and after" between potentiality and action occupied Aristotle a good deal. But that would lead us too far afield.

action (*energeia*) does not terminate when it reaches its end. For its *terminus a quo* is the same as its *terminus ad quem,* and the first on reaching perfection in the second survives as potentiality which demands new actualization.

We readily understand that Aristotle trembled when he first caught sight of a mode of being so desperately difficult to grasp.

For a rough illustration of the phenomenon let us consider the syllogism. The syllogism is an intellectual movement in which several "acts" of thinking are performed. But these "acts" are inseparable and belong to one unified thought. In thinking the first premise, we already stand in the unity of "syllogism" because we think the premise *as* a premise. This first act anticipates the entire syllogism but not its parts as such. These parts—that is, the second premise and the conclusion—are potentially present in the first premise. The second and the third "act" of thinking are thus the actualization of this potential content. But the second "act" in its turn reabsorbs and potentializes the first by referring to it as to a presupposition and thus preserving it. The third "act" behaves in the same way toward the first and the second. Thus thinking constantly transforms into actuality what had previously been in it in the form of potentiality, and again reabsorbs and transforms into potentiality what had previously existed *in actu.*

The process may become clearer when we make use of another attribute of *potentiality* and *actuality.* Potentiality is the possibility of being or not being, and it also is the possibility of being this or being that. Consequently it is an indeterminate being. Elimination of one of the alternatives results in final determination of the potentiality, which thus becomes plenary, operative, actual being. The movement "thinking" is a determining itself, and that gives it the character of a "progress toward itself." In the syllogism, we witness this process of the progressive self-determination of thinking.

If we now regard the totality of the philosophical quest from the Greeks to this day as an immense unified thinking, it presents itself as a process of self-determination in which the past is preserved and integrated—that is, as a thinking in progress toward itself.

I cannot resist seizing the opportunity and emphasizing the enormous importance of the discovery made by Aristotle in his effort to comprehend the movement that is thinking. It seemed to him that he beheld being from within. The being of all other things may appear static. The very changes and movements of bodies seemingly end in a state of fixed being. But the being of the reality thinking is not repose, not a stable figure, but a making-itself, an incessant engendering. Here "to be" acquires the value of an active verb, of exercising and operating. The static conception of being, so characteristic of Greek thinking, is changed by this man, who came from the outskirts of the Hellenic world, into a dynamic conception of being. Henceforth the standard example of being will not be furnished by the geometrical figure, which is pure aspect or spectacle; being will come to denote the effort of something to maintain itself in existence.[30]

The concept of energetic being triumphs over the concept of static being.

But we stand here at the extreme limit to which the Greek mind was able to advance in this realm. The vision of operative being comes and goes before Aristotle's eye with a curious rhythm. He is unable to grasp it firmly, let alone to use it as the foundation of his whole system.

The different varieties of movement proper—alteration, quan-

[30] The other instances of "action" given by Aristotle are: to see, to be happy, to love, to live. They, too, are movements that have their ends in themselves. They all belong to the domain of human phenomena; they are "visions from within."

My reader must not be discouraged if he does not at once understand this commentary to an Aristotelian text. What I want to convey comes down to this: the customary and obvious explanation of "potential being" starts from the concept of "actual or plenary being." Whereas I maintain that the best part of the concept "action" escapes us unless we approach it from the notion of potentiality and realize that "actualization" implies potentiality as such. I am surprised to find that, although Aristotle's philosophy is frequently called dynamic, no one has ever drawn the obvious conclusion that the decisive point in his idea of reality is the *dynamis*—namely, the potentiality—and not, as may first appear, the simple "actuality" seen from without and deprived of its implications.

titative change, locomotion—are finite because they terminate
on reaching their end. Their end is also their conclusion. But
action, *energeia,* is a continuous movement and in that sense
infinite.[31] If we say that a movement has terminated when it has
reached its end, thinking—and *energeia* in general—has terminated from the beginning. But because here the end is the
very act of thinking, the movement must begin afresh in an infinite revolving about itself, an infinite actualization of possibility—which is what we call reality. It is this process that will
in the course of the philosophical quest appear as the "monad"
of Leibnitz, the "transcendental *ego*" of Kant, Hegel's "*Geist,*"
Schopenhauer's "will," the "*élan vital*" of Bergson.

Aristotle's alternating avoidance of, and relapse into, the concept of static being is revealed by the duality of terms he em-
ploys for complete being—*energeia* and *entelecheia. Entelecheia* is being as the static and immutable end of the movement
by which it is produced—τέλος being the aim; whereas *energeia*
is the movement that, on terminating in itself, cannot help
beginning anew. Who travels for the sake of traveling must,
when he arrives at the inn, depart again. And such are living
and being. The *entelecheia* preserves within Aristotle's philosophical system the visual conception of being—being as aspect,
figure, and spectacle—which Aristotle took over from Plato;
whereas *energeia* is destined to become the modern concept par
excellence. We read in Goethe: *Im Anfang war die Tat.* And in
Fichte: *Sein ist reine Bewegung.*

HISTORY HAS ENDS BUT NO END

Hegel and Comte [32] were the first to rehabilitate the past
which theretofore, being stigmatized as pure error, had been

---

[31] I may here repeat what I have said about the revolution of the heavens as
an intermediary phenomenon between movement proper and action. The idea
of being as "continuous motion" will always make Aristotelism the opposite of
modern physics. As Einstein once told me: "Physics is the way of apprehending
phenomena that avoids continuous motion."

[32] Of course there are also Condorcet and Turgot who first descried something
like progress in history.

deprived of its right of ever having existed. Both Hegel and Comte construct history as an evolution in which every epoch forms an irreplaceable step to an end and as such possesses absolute meaning and full truth of its own. The historical perspective is inverted and now results in a history that was infallibly right; error does not exist. The new conception is due to the fact that Hegel and Comte arrange the evolutionary process of the human past in view of an *absolute* goal, a final philosophy which is their respective doctrine. But with such procedure they freeze history and bring it to a standstill, as Joshua did with the sun when he bade it stay upon Gibeon.

A philosophy that is called final is taken out of the historical process and made timeless. In this lies the limitation of the first guise under which the "historical sense" made its appearance. Hegel and Comte succeeded in detecting a meaning in the past, but at the cost of relating the past to something ultrahistorical, a *pléroma* or "fulfillment of all times" which in so far as it is fulfillment ceases to be in time.

To conceive an evolution in view of an absolute and determinate end is naturalism; such an evolution has its place in botany, zoology, and embryology. Since the fully developed shape of the living organism is known beforehand, all preliminary stages may be arranged as steps that lead to the complete state.

Our vision of history is very different from Hegel's and Comte's. We do not, and we need not, hold our own philosophy to be final. We see it embedded in the stream of history like any other perishable product of the ages. That means we regard *every* philosophy as essentially faulty, ours like the rest. But faulty or not, a philosophy is all it ought to be as long as it represents the authentic way of thinking proper to the epoch and the philosophical mind from which it sprang. The historical perspective changes again: Like the eighteenth century we maintain that the past is a history of errors, but now with a connotation that has little to do with the absolutism of eighteenth-century historians. To them all earlier thinking seemed erroneous because they were sure to possess the final truth; the errors of the past became absolute errors in clashing with the absolute truth. We, however, who believe that what is called truth always implies a larger or smaller dose of error—that error which each epoch is entitled, nay bound, to commit—we know that we mean no disparagement of the past when we say that history is the history of errors. Those errors were "necessary errors"—necessary in various senses, but above all because former epochs had to commit them so that we may avoid them.[33]

The present calls for the past; and *that is why* a philosophy is *the* true philosophy not when it is final—an inconceivable thing —but when it holds within itself as its vital organs all past philosophies, recognizing them as "progress toward itself." In this sense philosophy is history of philosophy, and vice versa.

Here we see philosophy share in the fundamental feature of all human occupation: to be a promise that is never fulfilled. Man's doing is found wanting, and it would be vain to expect of him full realization.

This, then, is how history of philosophy is set up with a view to an end: our philosophy, which is not ultimate but as historical and perishable as any other of its kind in the past. Our philosophy becomes, of itself, a link in the Bacchic chain—"all members of which are drunk," as Hegel said—and reaches out to future links, announcing, demanding, and preparing them.

In the caravans that cross the parched deserts of Libya we have heard an old adage which says: "Drink from the well and make room for the next."

[33] We cannot here properly elucidate this grave subject because that would require an exposition of our "theory of truth" in which the concept of "truth"— and that of "error" correspondingly—has acquired a rather unorthodox meaning.

*A Chapter from
the History of Ideas—
Wilhelm Dilthey*
AND
the Idea of Life

Contents

INTRODUCTION

AS THE name of Wilhelm Dilthey is likely to meet with small response except in German circles, we may begin these pages with informing the reader that Dilthey is a philosopher; moreover, that he is the most important philosopher in the second half of the nineteenth century. So great a discrepancy between the rank of a man and the ring of a name, though not uncommon in history, always implies a certain abnormality. Indeed, that Dilthey should have remained comparatively unknown outside the German intellectual sphere is due to the fact that even within it considerable time elapsed before his stature emerged with a distinctness concordant with the actual value of his work.

But the interesting—and somewhat more than interesting—feature about Dilthey is that his was certainly not a light hid under a bushel. From 1882 to 1911 he held a chair of philosophy at the University of Berlin as successor to no one less than Lotze. A member of the Prussian Academy, head of a whole philosophical school, held in high esteem among the most consequential persons in German science and education, he was indeed by no external and accidental circumstances denied a position favorable to the full exercise of his influence.

The dimness of his figure and his tardy appreciation are due to deep and essential reasons ultimately rooted in his own doctrine—so much so that to propound Dilthey's thinking and to point out the causes of his limited influence and late triumph are one and the same.

This twofold purpose has inspired the following pages. Therein an excellent opportunity will be offered to catch a glimpse of the subtle process called history of ideas—the royal march of human thinking. Our concern here will be with that great Idea which has of late appeared on this earth and wrought its mysterious and all but magical work upon us. This Idea with a capital I—for capital it is itself—must be distinguished from common ideas which may or may not come into a man's head, it being a matter of chance whether the concepts in an individual mind fall into just this pattern. But an Idea of this supreme order cannot fail to be conceived, for it is a necessary form of human destiny and an evolutionary stage at which mankind inexorably arrives after having exhausted the preceding stages. Stoicism, rationalism, idealism, positivism are such Ideas. But then it hardly makes sense to say that such an Idea is in this or that man, that it has occurred to him. Rather it is men who from a certain moment on abide in it. All they do, think, and feel emanates, whether they know it or not, from that basic inspiration which forms the historical ground on which they move, the atmosphere in which they breathe, the substance they are. That is why the name of such an Idea matrix comes to denote an epoch.

The new great Idea in which man is beginning to abide is the Idea of life. Dilthey was among its first discoverers, but he still moved on that unknown ground with all the toil and trouble that fall to the lot of the pioneer. This study will make it clear that, strictly speaking, Dilthey never knew that he had arrived at a new continent, and never succeeded in taking possession of the land on which he trod. For fifty years he stretched out his hands in untiring effort to catch that fleeting vision of the Idea that had flashed upon him in his early youth. In vain. The Idea, which at its first appearance had seemed so easy to lay hands on, proved more and more elusive to any attempt at capture by clear concepts. Was it Dilthey's own incapacity as a thinker? Was it the ever recurrent tragedy that the first appearance of an Idea is *always* premature and that the thinker witnessing it— like him "who saw too young the perfect beauty"—labors under the terrible anachronism of having to think the new Idea with the ideas of his time, that is, with ideas born of another and moribund Idea? All these questions to which we are to find an answer will put the reader on the track of why a study on Dilthey may yield some insight into that secret fermentation which is the history of ideas—one of the fundamental dimensions of the history of man.

Never before has it happened that the advent of a great Idea was witnessed by a generation possessed of historical vision. In full command of a clear historical sense, we are in our time witnessing the birth of an epoch. Unhampered as we are by the problematic intervention of documents and testimonies—for this uncommon event has been occurring within ourselves and in our immediate past, a past recorded in a still living memory, not yet in archives—we ought to be able to rectify some of the current notions of historical methodology.

For an instance let us mention the principle that the historian must, for any idea belonging to a certain time, find its source or, more accurately, that he must look for the direct, precise, and unquestionable influence exercised by one individual—either personally or through his work—upon another individual. Here we have a regulative principle of unassailable strength and one that represents the condition on which the possibility of historical science depends. The minds of men do not throw up sudden stray ideas without ancestors or precedents. History is perfect continuity. Every idea of mine springs from another idea of mine or of someone else, and in its turn gives birth to further ideas. There is no spontaneous generation. *Omnis cellula e cellula.* "Coming from" and "going toward" are constitutive characteristics of ideas. Like rivers—to use a most apposite hydraulic metaphor—they have a source and a mouth.

But the question is whether this principle holds good for great Ideas. Does their concrete appearance in an individual mind necessarily presuppose a likewise individual and concrete source? Indeed, when a great Idea has fully matured and rules over an epoch through impregnation, nobody thinks any longer of pointing out a definite source for the expression this Idea finds in a definite book. The triumphant and valid Idea is omnipresent; it is the epoch itself; individuals, as we were saying, live in the Idea rather than the Idea in them. That the same thing also and particularly happens in the initial stages of an

Idea, I need not be told by other people. For in the advent of the Idea of life I was involved myself, and I know that I received it, and could have received it, from no alien source. I am, furthermore, convinced that none of the four or five other original discoverers relied on any thinking but his own. To confirm and explain this surprising fact is the objective of the following pages. Let me summarize them in these four statements which may seem exaggerated and paradoxical but are not:

1. Dilthey's writings, a work of genius, have served little or not at all to promote the subsequent advances in the conception of the Idea of life.

2. On the contrary, those independent advances have lent to Dilthey's thought meaning and importance which without them and by itself it would be lacking. Thus we here have the case of an idea carrying water to its "source."

3. The same strange relation must always have prevailed in the initial stages of a great Idea. The reason being that the elements or ingredients of a great Idea range over an enormous area. If they did not, they would not cover the universal problem in its totality and could not modify human life in all its aspects. But it is not easy for a man to succeed single-handed in opening his angle of vision wide enough to behold all the disparate elements. Great Ideas come into existence piecemeal, each of their several aspects being descried independently by such individuals as have an angle of vision kindred with it. Once all its elements are brought to light, the Idea constitutes itself as one whole which now seems extremely simple.

4. The true and only source benefiting the initiators of an Idea is the intellectual level that has been reached in the course of human evolution. That is why the several pieces of the Idea are discovered by people who live far apart and do not know each other. All they have in common is that they stand on the same level in the scale of mankind's experiences.[1]

[1] For an example of the tangles from which this rectification of historical method may save the historian, let us consider the endless discussions centering around the question whether or not the Cartesian *Cogito* has its origin in St. Augustine. Again, the point at issue is the rise of a great Idea: idealistic ration-

CHANCE, FATE, CHARACTER

"Life is a mysterious fabric woven of chance, fate, and character," [2] Dilthey wrote toward the end of his long life, a life spent in indefatigable meditation on the secret of human life in

---

alism. There have been coming to light more and more coincidences of expression between Descartes and the Father of the Church with regard to the fundamental problem of the existence of the "I." But at the same time it becomes ever clearer that their respective philosophical theses are entirely different. The one thing truly uniting Descartes with St. Augustine lies so deep that it does not appear explicitly in any thesis or formulation of either of them. Historians have either not seen or not dared to state that Descartes' philosophy as such—not the man Descartes but his formal doctrine—is the continuation of the Christian doctrine and presupposes the great human experience that is Christianism. But this Christianism, Descartes' "source," is certainly not the particular doctrine of St. Augustine or St. Anselm or this or that Father of the Church. On the other hand, to call St. Augustine the source, in the strict sense, of the *Cogito*, which is a particular though decisive thesis within the Cartesian system, is ridiculous and will be only the more so the more major coincidences of terms appear. To refute this derivation, let us call to mind that St. Augustine's words had been there, accessible to all, for about thirteen centuries before they gave rise—what a chance!—to the *Cogito* in the 1620's.

Another instance of this kind of methodological error—although in a matter of lesser magnitude—is furnished by the question whether Aristarchus of Samos can be regarded as the source of Copernicus. Unlike Descartes—great eraser of his own traces—the admirable canon collected in his book all earlier opinions bearing resemblance to his own. Yet here again the eighteen centuries separating Aristarchus from Copernicus clearly show that the Copernican system was not influenced by Aristarchus' idea, but on the contrary exercised what may be called an influence on it.

In bursting upon the world, great inventions produce an effect not only forward but also backward; they influence the past by drawing an echo from it. This possibility of retroaction, which in the physical realm does not exist except metaphorically, forms an essential characteristic of historical causality. Life, which is a perpetual creation of the future, is at the same time a perpetual reforming of the past. The past as such lives differently in different epochs.

History, even more than physics, is the science of causation and, like physics, it investigates nothing if not causal relations. What is not a process of effectuation has no historical reality; any more than what does not give rise to a function has physical reality. Hence equality of two ideas means nothing in history. Apart from and beyond such equality it must be shown that, and how decisively, the two ideas influenced one another. As regards Copernicus and Descartes, it is clear that for their discoveries the doctrines of Aristarchus and St. Augustine respectively are of negligible import and that if it had not been for other true causes those ancient formulations would not have given new birth at just those moments.

[2] Wilhelm Dilthey, *Gesammelte Schriften, op. cit.*, vol. VII, p. 74.

general. It is impossible to unravel now in one stroke all that this sentence signifies and implies. This is the difference between philosophical and literary expression: that the latter is expansive and prone to pour out before the reader or hearer its entire signification, nay more than it properly signifies, which it clearly could not do if it were packed with meaning of a very precise sort. Philosophical expression, on the other hand, is hermetic. Even in the most favorable case of the most lucid thinker the little doors of the sentences are firmly shut, their meaning does not step out on its own feet. To comprehend them, there is no means but to enter. Yet once inside, we understand the reason for this strange condition of philosophical sentences which, being expression—and that means a saying—are also, and more, silence and secrecy. Philosophical thought is systematic, and in a system each concept carries all the others within it. But language can at one moment say only a few things; it cannot say them all at once. It is discourse, a going on saying and never having finished saying. Philosophical sentences cannot be expansive, for they are essentially inclusive. In this they are like love and great grief which, when striving to become manifest in words, seem to choke the throat with the avalanche of all that should be said. Love and great grief in their way are systems also and disciplines, therefore, of silence and secrecy.

For the time being this sentence of Dilthey's serves only as a bowsprit behind which to set forth on our long and complicated voyage. It stands here as a symbol for that portion of the present study which is intended to pay homage to this admirable thinker. And the homage consists in conducting our search on the history of ideas—the perpetual theme of Dilthey's work—in a spirit which, I think, would have pleased him. That is why I begin—anyone not familiar with Dilthey's work may be startled by such a beginning—with an autobiographical remark.

I became acquainted with Dilthey's work as late as 1929, and it took me four more years before I knew it sufficiently well. This ignorance, I do not hesitate to maintain, has caused me to lose about ten years of my life—ten years, in the first place, of intellectual development, but that, of course, means an equal loss in all other dimensions of life.

Was this due to chance; did it form part of my destiny; or was it the doing of my character? That is what we are going to see. But for the reader's orientation let me state in advance that what happened to me, in varying degree and in a more or less palpable form, happened to all of us. What I have in mind, expressed in a schematic form, is this: The intellectual life of present-day Europe depends on the tempo with which the idea of life is developed.[3] But this development has been delayed by about a decade because the thinkers who might have accelerated it were late in coming upon the work of Dilthey. Now, if this is so, it was not entirely their own fault—that is, owing to their character; nor was it mere chance. In this most unfortunate tardiness, there intervened as a decisive factor the very necessity of things, hence destiny.

At whatever point we enter into historical reality with a mind to understanding it, the first thing we run into is chance. Chance forms the surface, the skin, of historical reality.

When I studied in Berlin in 1906 none of the philosophical chairs of the university was occupied by an outstanding scholar. Dilthey *happened* to have given up lecturing in the university building a few years before and admitted to the courses he held in his home only a few specially prepared students. Thus *chance* had it that I did not come in touch with him. However, I wanted to get acquainted with his work. But what was his work? Well, this: A stout volume of purely historical content written in his youth, *Leben Schleiermachers* (Life of Schleiermacher), 1870 —a first volume never followed by a second. The first volume —also without a second—of his cardinal work *Einleitung in die Geisteswissenschaften* (Introduction into the Humanities), 1883. A few articles, very important but unfinished and seemingly of a historical nature, on the ideas prevailing in the Renaissance and the seventeenth century; others on the eighteenth century in

---

[3] In which exact sense we may say that historical reality depends on this or that event—that is, on a particular cause—must here remain unexplained.

Germany, published in *Archiv für Geschichte der Philosophie*, 1890. Half a dozen papers, fragmentary, too, which had been read in the meetings of the Prussian Academy and were published in *Sitzungsberichte der Königlich Preussischen Akademie der Wissenschaften*.[4] Lastly a book on history of literature *Das Erlebniss und die Dichtung* (Experience and Poetry), 1905.

Those were the most important works Dilthey had published up to 1906. Was there much more to come? A not too voluminous study on the essence of philosophy, *Das Wesen der Philosophie*, 1909. Another even shorter one, *Typen der Weltanschauung und ihre Entwicklung in den metaphysischen Systemen* (Types of World Vision and Their Development in the Metaphysical Systems), 1911. And three or four papers read before the Prussian Academy, with which we will deal later.

Dilthey's historical studies are perhaps the best work ever done in history—in the eyes of those who are in the secret of his thinking. Those who are not will see in them nothing but more or less useful studies on philosophical sources. In his properly philosophical writings, Dilthey uses an ethereal, elusive language, while in his historical work he almost exasperatingly refrains from mentioning the systematic foundations from which those studies arise and derive their meaning. His historical studies were to him mere fragments destined to acquire their full meaning only after having been assigned their place in the projected whole.

Nor did the papers published in *Sitzungsberichte der Preussischen Akademie* convey the mainspring of his philosophy. At that time, they were deemed mere psychology, fine, subtle, thorough, important, but no more. And this, as we shall see later, was what, in a way, they meant to Dilthey himself.

---

[4] The titles of the three principal papers are: *Beiträge zur Lösung der Frage vom Ursprung unseres Glaubens an die Realität der Aussenwelt und seinem Recht* (Contributions to the Solution of the Problem Concerning Origin and Right of Our Belief in the Reality of the Outer World), 1890. *Ideen über eine beschreibende und zergliedernde Psychologie* (Ideas for a Descriptive and Analytic Psychology), 1894. *Beiträge zum Studium der Individualität* (Contributions to the Study of Individuality), 1895–1896.

There thus remained for the young student of 1906 no other way of entering into Dilthey's fundamental thought than to study his *Introduction into the Humanities*. But I could not read that book, either. Already out of print for many years, it *happened* to be one of the rarest contemporary books on the market. Many times I tried to procure it from the university library, but thanks to its rareness it always *happened* to be out. Moreover, now after having read it I know that, as regards the main point, my studying it in 1906 would have been useless for the simple reason that the *Introduction* is solely a beginning and not an adequate exposition of Dilthey's thought.

At this point the reader will have formed two entirely correct impressions and which I intended to provoke: first that there is too much chance, and second that there is much to be amazed at about Dilthey's production, at least when considered, as it ought to be considered, as the expression of a philosopher's philosophy.[5] The two come down to one simple fact: Dilthey never adequately propounded his thought in public. Only now after the posthumous publication, in the *Collected Writings*, of his attempts at an exposition in personal notes and first drafts found among his papers is it possible to gain a clear idea of the decisive trends of his thinking. Theretofore his inspiring influence did not reach beyond the very small circle of his immediate pupils.

Let us then make the last observation but one. The so-called chance that prevented me from becoming acquainted with Dilthey's thinking in time now looks more like a natural consequence of the inadequate form in which it was conveyed by his published work. This is the real reason why not only I but all others who might have used his inspiration toward a speedier development of the Idea of life failed by *chance*—owing to this or that anecdotical circumstance—to come in time under Dilthey's influence. The mere fact that Max Scheler, a man with a

[5] None of Dilthey's works has yet been translated into English. Professor H. A. Hodges' book *Wilhelm Dilthey*, Kegan Paul, 1945, which contains long excerpts from Dilthey, is the first to introduce Dilthey to the English-speaking world (*translator's note*).

frenetic curiosity and the keen flair of a setter for everything intellectually important, should have unsuspectingly passed Dilthey by excuses me from adding further data and reasons. On the contrary, a chance coincidence it would have been to belong to the very small group of Dilthey's intimate pupils—the only way of being let into his secret and stirred by his way of thinking.

And now to the last point. That Dilthey should never have advanced his own idea wholly or at least adequately—the cause of all these alleged *chances*—did not come about by *chance*, either. *It is characteristic of Dilthey that he never succeeded in thinking through to the end, in shaping and mastering, his own intuition.* Even his son-in-law and closest pupil, Georg Misch, is obliged, in the beginning of one of his two studies dedicated to the master, to admit "the fragmentary character" of Dilthey's work, if only in that "his reflections on his own endeavors and intentions . . . are wanting in logical clarity and have not throughout consolidated into radical and adequately rendering concepts. What is seemingly fragmentary and in fact unfinished in his work can be traced back to that point—the thorny point of all philosophy—where *intuitio* must be carried over into *ratio*." [6] That is why he exercised "only after his death an influence beyond the circle of his immediate pupils, and even that was slow in coming." [7]

In the pursuit of his own idea Dilthey stopped midway. Hence the lack of fullness and precision, of cogency in all his formulations. It would be pointless to discuss them if we left them in their own inadequacy. We cannot expound ideas prior to our own thought unless we have understood them better than did their author, and that is possible only when we have gone beyond him.[8] Such having gone beyond is the presupposition as

[6] Cf. the Preface in Dilthey, *op. cit.*, vol. V, p. xii (1924).

[7] Georg Misch, *Die Philosophie des Lebens und die Phänomenologie*, 1930, p. 1.

[8] This assertion, indicative not of presumption but of an obligation, falls in line with one of the central ideas of Dilthey's hermeneutics.

well as the imperative of all history. Thus on the threshold of this study the reader had better be forewarned that in this case expounding is completing.

But it may well be that the falling short of its own measure characteristic of Dilthey's thinking is not so rare as it first seems. The same, I dare say, happened to every thinker who initiated the evolution of a great Idea; and immediate successors always went through the kind of experiences that my generation suffered with respect to Dilthey.

When at last I became acquainted with Dilthey's philosophical work I was struck by a strange and disconcerting parallelism between his ideas and the problems and positions, of a strictly and decisively philosophical character, set forth in my own writings. From my first book *Meditations on Don Quixote* (1914) to *The Revolt of the Masses* (1929) this parallelism manifests itself with Arcadian candor. Why, then, complain that my intellectual development was retarded by ten years because I did not know Dilthey? Did not this simply mean that I had arrived on my own at the same ideas that he had already discovered and set down? What could I have gained by taking them over from him? No, the question is not one of taking over ideas. It is somewhat more complicated.

The fact is that there are in my work hardly any ideas that coincide with or even presuppose Dilthey's. Exactly that is what I deplore. That is what made me lose ten years. Moreover, my problems and positions belong, from the first, to a stage in the evolution of the idea of life beyond that of Dilthey.

And the parallelism? Parallelism precisely excludes coincidence; it signifies exact correspondence. Parallels do not touch each other, because they start at different points. Their converging in the infinite expresses the contradiction that they are at once the same and most different. Only two parallel lines of thinking can be certain never to coincide materially, for they are separated by a most radical difference, that of a distinct starting point. They *tackle the problem on different levels,* one more advanced and plenary than the other. With respect to the problem of life, *living reason* marks a higher level than *historical reason* at which Dilthey came to a halt.

Meanwhile the work accomplished by Dilthey on his own level is admirable. It is distinguished by the erudition and workmanship characteristic of one who has fallen heir to a magnificent philosophical tradition. By historical necessity, his work represented a presupposition of my work, and this presupposition I was late in discovering. Not that there is much in Dilthey that could have actually been used for working out the pivotal terms of living reason, but to have gone through his discipline would have meant a lot. Many perplexities and fruitless attempts might have been saved, and the idea of living reason would have found support and confirmation at the right moment. For to feed on what will, in the end, be discharged is one of the fundamental laws of life.

Here ends the autobiographical preamble which will, however, orient the reader on the tangled roads ahead more than he now expects. Indeed, it is perhaps not quite so personal and casual as it now appears; it may, for aught we know, hold exemplary value. At the dawn of a new Idea things must always have happened in some similar way.

THE HISTORICAL SCHOOL

The fact that, in the world of intellectual relations, a man like Dilthey existed but was, to all intents and purposes, as good as nonexistent—this paradoxical character of absence inflicted upon his presence—calls for a thorough explanation. For to all this we must yet add the final stroke. Not only did Dilthey's influence not reach beyond his immediate pupils, but his pupils, on their part, are characterized by a strange incapacity for setting up a clear-cut body of doctrine and for exercising influence on their surroundings. This as it were maimed condition of a whole school cannot be passed over in silence, because it serves better than anything else to impart to readers entirely unfamiliar with Dilthey's case a feeling for the highly abnormal historical role played by this great thinker.

Our task is to make this abnormality intelligible by pointing out its roots, on the one hand, in the specific situation of the epoch in which Dilthey lived and thought, and, on the other, in the conditions of his character and style—style of thought and of expression. But any such attempt at clarification must remain in mid-air, carrying no conviction unless it begins with an exposition of Dilthey's fundamental idea. His fundamental idea is of supreme simplicity, only it needs a brief preparation.

Dilthey, son of a Protestant clergyman, begins his university work as a student of theology. But as he has no true religious belief, study of religion turns for him into study of history. It is the time of the great German historians and philologists. In such an environment his vocation for history asserts itself decisively.

"When I came to Berlin around 1850—how long ago and how few remain of those then living—the great movement culminated in which the science of history and through it the sciences of the humanities in general finally took shape. The seventeenth century produced the mathematical sciences of nature through an unequaled collaboration of the cultured peoples of that time. The setting up of the historical sciences has originated in Germany, it had its center here in Berlin, and I had the inestimable good fortune to live and study here in that period." [9]

Dilthey read with, or met, Bopp, the founder of comparative linguistics; Boeckh, the great philologist; Jakob Grimm; Mommsen; the geographer Ritter; Ranke; Treitschke. Together with the preceding generation of Wilhelm von Humboldt, Savigny, Niebuhr, Eichhorn, those distinguished scholars formed the famous *Historische Schule*. The work of the Historical School marks the first encounter of scientific consciousness with a strange and theretofore unnoticed form or region of reality: the

---

[9] Dilthey, *op. cit.*, vol. V, p. 7. From a speech made to an intimate circle of friends and pupils at the celebration of his seventieth birthday.

reality that is human life. Now what do we mean by intimating that this reality, which is man himself, had gone unnoticed up to that time? Had the people before 1800 not been aware that they were living? Of course they had, since to live is precisely to be aware that one lives, to be present at what happens to oneself. But my being present at my own life is a very different thing from recognizing that this life of mine, together with the lives of all men past and present, forms a peculiar reality on a par with the reality of stars or the reality of organisms. My awareness of my life in living it does not present my life to me as an object that is there outside myself like rocks or trees and that, because of its being there outside myself (of its being an objective reality) I can and must study in its peculiar texture as I study rocks or trees. The primary intimacy that I have with my life while I am living it prevents me from seeing it as an object and a reality capable of becoming a theme of investigation and a problem for reason. Our lives are transparent to us, and what is transparent is hardest to see. We are in general better in observing the outer world which, being outside, is opaque, unknown, and perplexing. It is not for nothing that in the word "strange" the meaning of the *ethymon—extraneus* or outside—appears tinged with that of "puzzling." Before a thing becomes an object of cognition it must have been a problem, and before it becomes a problem we must have found it strange.

From the days of Greece down to the eighteenth century, history is narration. The life of humankind, past and contemporary, is told as one tells one's own. The narrative may be more or less exact and elaborate—in Thucydides and Polybius it is both to a very respectable degree—but the fundamental attitude of the historian is that of a storyteller. Now narration implies that the narrated events are essentially clear and not problematic. In this it is of the same kind with the spontaneous recording that forms part of our immediate personal existence. It also resembles this recording in that it dwells not on human life as such but only on its extraordinary parts: war and pestilence, kings, statesmen, generals, and prodigies.

Before man could begin to wonder at human life and understand it to be a reality in its own right, he had to be possessed of an exact and rigorous system of cosmic reality and have true knowledge of the consistency of material phenomena. The triumph, in Newton's work, of a mechanical interpretation of the physical world necessarily entailed attempts to subject all reality to the same procedure. Consequently, at the end of the seventeenth and throughout the eighteenth century, thinkers in England and France tried to apply the scientific method to human phenomena. And it was in the course of those endeavors that the obstinate resistance of human phenomena to mechanical interpretation paved the way for the discovery of human life as a reality in its own right—a reality no less, nay more, opaque than the cosmic reality had been. By that time nature had, at last, become intelligible; it had, moreover, acquired the character of exemplary intelligibility and had, in principle, ceased to be problematic. The recalcitrance of human phenomena against scientific treatment won attention for them and secured to them the character of a reality proper. It is surprising yet undeniable that no thing is deemed a reality save in proportion to its being obstinate.

As is the rule with such great experiences of mankind, one thinker—Giambattista Vico—anticipated the new reality in a grandiose but sleepwalking vision. In one dash he went beyond all his eighteenth-century successors; but his insight was like a dream or a nightmare.[10] The full and thorough conquest of the new continent was yet to cost the efforts of a century and a half. As Copernicus was succeeded by Tycho Brahe, the genius of precision in measurement, so Vico was succeeded by the Frenchman Bayle, that microscope of historical criticism. And as after Tycho comes Kepler, so after Bayle, Voltaire. I will not press

[10] Vico's influence reached its full scope only a century later. But it also took fifty years before the influence of Copernicus made itself felt.

the parallel; but the correspondence in the order of those great discoveries in physics and in history respectively is so suggestive that the former may serve to clarify the latter.

Kepler was the first not to impose upon the metric data of star positions the preconceived idea of a form, the circle, which had been favored by scientists for purely subjective reasons. He understood that the problem must be inverted, that astronomy must start from data and search for the form reality is pleased to possess. Something similar was done by Voltaire. He was the first who did not identify historical reality with major catastrophes, battles, and the political plottings of courts and assemblies. To him it was clear that the substantive form of human life is of a different kind. Human life is more; prior to all this, it is daily routine. Life is "customs and spirit"—modes of feeling, thinking, desiring, interweaving to form the hourly and daily background of historical time against which the glamor of those other patterns stands out in relief. In his *Essai sur les moeurs et l'esprit des nations,* Voltaire wrote a history that has definitely ceased to be a chronicle—that is, a narrative of more or less extraordinary events.[11]

As Kepler's work is chronologically interlaced with that of Galileo, so Voltaire's is with that of Montesquieu. Kepler and Voltaire discover the form of physical and historical reality respectively. But Occidental man, in contrast with the Greeks, has never been satisfied with forms. He wants to comprehend why a form is what it is, and therefore seeks the generating and maintaining forces behind it—its mechanism, its dynamism. It is this that Galileo adds to Kepler, and Montesquieu to Voltaire. Montesquieu is the first to interpret historical phenomena dynamically; he conceives human life as made, in its ultimate reality, not of fixed patterns but of acting impulses—the monarchical form of government being the manifestation and result of "honor" in action, the republican of "virtue" in action. Honor

---

[11] Cf. Ernst Cassirer, *Die Philosophie der Aufklärung,* 1932, p. 297, and also Dilthey's own study "Das 18. Jahrhundert und die historische Welt," in *op. cit.,* vol. III, pp. 209–268.

and virtue are pure agents; when their impetus dwindles and dies, monarchy and republic decline and fall.

But Montesquieu's dynamic theory explains forms only in their present tense. He is blind to the decisively historical quality of human forms: their arising from one another, their transformation. Human life is incessant metamorphosis. Each human form appears at a definite place in the sequence in which the forms follow one another in time. There is no "historical consciousness" unless each form is seen in its time perspective, at its own place in historical time, rising from previous forms, giving rise to subsequent ones. In other words, human reality is evolutionary, and investigation of it has to proceed genetically. In Turgot, Condorcet, and Lessing, the new day of the science of history arises magnificently with the interpretation of the historical process as an evolution.

Already the prerequisites are there for man to think historically and to recognize the puzzling peculiarity of the reality that is he, over against the reality of matter. At this point, the Historical School begins its work.[12]

With his accustomed compact brevity, Dilthey has explained the meaning of this work in the atmosphere of which his mind was shaped. Dilthey, we must not fail to state, was the first to recognize, or rather to discover, that it is erroneous to put the eighteenth century down for an antihistorical epoch. On the contrary, it was, as we have seen, in the course of that century that one after another the component parts of historical vision were worked out. But the eighteenth century, while bringing forth the components, did not succeed in putting them together and in actually exercising the new mode of seeing for which it had paved the way. One cause there was which prevented eighteenth-century thinkers from dedicating themselves fully and unreservedly to the study of historical phenomena as such.

---

[12] To round out the picture, mention ought to be made of the contribution of the English historians Hume and Gibbon. In fact, the English wrote more concrete histories than the French, but their discoveries were less decisive. To sketch the process with as few lines as possible, I therefore refrain from speaking of them, although Hume in particular would deserve a very careful study.

And here we come upon the grain of truth in the summary
verdict on the eighteenth century as antihistorical. <u>The eighteenth century was faithful to its master the seventeenth in cling-
ing to the conviction that man ultimately possesses a "nature,"</u>
a definite, permanent, and <u>immutable</u> mode of being. Man in his
radical substance was believed to be "reason," and in so far as he
thinks, feels, desires rationally he is of no time and of no place.
Time and place but serve to shroud and thwart reason and to
hide from man his own rationality. <u>There exists a natural—that
is rational—religion identical with itself under all its historical
deformations</u>. There exist a natural law and an essential art and
a unique and immutable science. This means declaring that human "nature" is not historical in kind, and that historical forms
are, strictly speaking, deformations of man. This residue of
seventeenth-century mentality in the end undid "historical consciousness" in the very minds that had discovered it. Instead of
dwelling upon the human variety already lying open before
their eyes, they rushed on in search of substantive, immutable
man. The idea of historical forms, I repeat, had been conceived,
but historical forms were regarded as mere deformations of the
human substance. In the end there reappeared "the circle"—as
though Kepler had relapsed into Ptolemy.

But a mere elimination of this residue of rationalism will at
once disclose that "<u>the substance</u>" of man is precisely his muta-
ble and historical consistency. Man has no "nature"; he has history.[13] His being is not one but many and manifold, different
in each time and each place. To have been aware of this and to
have been engrossed in the kaleidoscopic spectacle of history,
describing its untold patterns and observing precisely their exclusive and stubborn peculiarities, is the achievement of the
Historical School. In it, as I have said above, <u>scientific consciousness is for the first time confronted with the human phenomenon
in its reality and not in its idealization</u>. Aristotle's man and Descartes' man is not a person we could meet and whom, because

[13] Cf. the article, "History as a System," in the author's book *Toward a Philosophy of History*, W. W. Norton and Co., 1940, p. 165.

we could meet him somewhere, we seem to see; he is an abstraction of such a person, a constructed idealization of such a person's sheer and full reality.

The Historical School took possession of this vast and virginal field of investigation not only in historiography but also in all properly human sciences: philosophy, philology and linguistics, literature, the sciences of law, state, and religion. In a short time, the entire past, mummified in documents, was revived. An immense amount of knowledge about human patterns and the modes and aspects of living reality was gathered. Thanks to the new way of seeing, a grandiose, never yet beheld spectacle came into sight—the glowing and infinitely picturesque pageantry of the multiform life of man.

But in the wealth and splendor of this panorama the Historical School got lost. Satisfied to see and to describe, rejecting intellectual construction as prone to do violence to reality and to behave antihistorically, those thinkers failed to give to their vision an adequate architecture. They doubtless succeeded in forging the exquisite formal tools required for dealing with such a subtle matter—the methods of textual criticism, of documentation, of linguistics, esthetics, and jurisprudence. Suffice it to mention again the names of Niebuhr, Savigny, Bopp, Boeckh, Ranke, Grimm.

But these methods, however important and indispensable, did not penetrate beyond the threshold of historical thinking proper. It is not enough to elucidate past events so that they can be discerned in their purity. History is not only seeing; it is thinking what has been seen. And in one sense or another, thinking is always construction. Owing to the inadequacy of, and even aversion against, construction, the Historical School—I quote Dilthey—"did not contrive such knowledge of the historico-social reality as may find exact expression in clear concepts and formulations, and thus become fruitful." Let us add that the fundamental concepts of the Historical School did not go beyond those set up by Vico, Voltaire, and Montesquieu. To give but one instance: what was Savigny's pivotal idea? That law, in the last analysis, is *Gewohnheitsrecht* (right founded on custom)—*moeurs,* Voltaire would say, and has its origin in *Volksgeist*—or *esprit des nations,* in Voltaire's terminology. In the end, the Historical School added no new principles to eighteenth-century thought; rather it was the result of a process of subtraction; it eliminated *reason.* Owing to its idiosyncrasy against construction, the Historical School degenerated into antiquarianism of an esthetic or a patriotic nature, into folklore and lore of customs.[14]

DILTHEY'S FUNDAMENTAL IDEA

It is at this point that Dilthey's fundamental idea takes its rise. I will develop it in my own way, using the text of his writings and strictly following the line of his thought but giving to his conception a somewhat more rounded and vigorous expression.

By the exigencies of his life, a man finds himself compelled to ponder upon what is the world; what is justice; what is the state; what society; what the beauty of the picture he paints or looks at; the music he composes or listens to; the language he uses. In asking thus, his aim is to find absolute answers to all these questions, and to discover what world, state, justice, society, beauty, language absolutely or in truth are. Such efforts toward the absolute are philosophy, the sciences of law and of state, sociology, esthetics and poetics, grammar.

But together with his urge to know the absolute truth in these matters, a man, since he lives in a time that has accumulated much historical knowledge, finds in himself a distinct notion that innumerable people before him have asked themselves the

---

[14] I find myself in this point in agreement with Count York, Dilthey's close friend. He writes, in *Briefwechsel zwischen Wilhelm Dilthey und Graf Paul York von Wartenburg,* 1923, p. 69: "The title 'Historical School' is a misnomer. This School was not historical but antiquarian; it constructed esthetically while the dominant tendency was that of mechanical construction." However, this sentence, like many others of the redoubtable Prussian, is profound, excessive, and misleading at once.

same questions and given themselves their absolute answers, trusting, for instance, wholeheartedly and without reservation, that the state is what they think it to be. Thus the absolutism of such "absolute" answers is canceled by their multiplicity. Why? The mere reason that they are many would not be sufficient; one might very well be absolutely true and all the others false. What happens is that these various opinions, in appearing side by side, act upon one another, and through their mutual criticism irrefutably demonstrate each the error of its neighbor.

The claim of each to have ascertained the absolute truth about world, state, society, beauty, language is convicted of error and voided. Faced with this recognition, ancient man found himself with no reality in his hands; he fell into radical skepticism.

But the generation that was in its twenties around 1850— Dilthey's generation—had inherited from two "idealistic" centuries the decisive insight that if someone is mistaken in what he thinks, the content of his thinking has no reality but there remains as a reality the intellectual fact that someone has thought this. And the same holds good with respect to feeling and desiring. Idealism has, once and for all, discovered and stated the unassailable reality of subjective phenomena.[15] But then idealism, in its turn, proceeds to erect upon this reality new absolute constructions. In so far as it advances absolute opinions on world, state, and so on, idealism, no less than any absolutism, is in error and can be accorded no other reality than that of the simple fact that someone holds these opinions. Skepticism left man empty-handed. Idealism, when foundering as absolutism, leaves to us as a reality the fact that someone at such and such a place and time thought, desired, felt in such and such a manner.

Thinking, then, gives up defining, at least directly, anything that claims to be absolute, and resolves to investigate the one

[15] The reader will discover between the lines of the present study a doctrine that goes beyond Dilthey's. This doctrine is by no means realistic; it recognizes all the truth residing in idealism. But the fact is that all the truth residing in idealism is not the whole truth.

and only reality unquestionably given to it: such subjective facts of thinking, desiring, feeling as have occurred at a certain time and a certain place—that is to say, historical facts. "Pure" or absolute thinking gives way to historical thinking.

Thus historical thinking proceeds in respect of human phenomena—philosophy, law, society, arts and letters, language, religion—as the natural sciences, when they were set up in the works of Kepler and Galileo, proceeded in respect of material phenomena. It is concerned with facts exclusively; it behaves empirically and is, at its face value, "positivism."

But physical "positivism," enjoying a start of three centuries, had succeeded in constructing a "system of nature" in which are integrated the exemplarily rigorous physico-mathematical sciences and around them the less exemplarily, but still very efficaciously, rigorous biological sciences. This body of knowledge holds, from the seventeenth century on, the rank of model knowledge. Philosophy bows to it and receives from it decisive orientations. Physics establishes itself as the prototype of truth. And as reason is nothing if not that conduct of thinking that leads to truth, reason becomes synonymous with "natural science."

What intellectual conduct had secured such unequaled triumph? This question forms the great theme of Kant, and it stirs again, after the interlude marked by the "romantic orgy" of Fichte, Schelling, and Hegel, around 1850. Physical reason or physico-mathematical method starts, it is true, from simple facts; but it does not end there. If it did, it would be lost in mere description of phenomena which, for their number and diversity, are an unfathomable ocean. Classical physics is not all observation. It implies mechanics—a nonempirical discipline of mathematical rigor [16] which, by constructing ideal bodies and deducting their laws of motion, furnishes a unique and unified scheme to which the bewildering multiformity of physical phenomena can be referred and thus ordered and reduced to a system.

[16] Cf. the author's study, "Hegel and Historiology," in *Revista de Occidente*, 1928.

The Historical School in the atmosphere of which Dilthey breathed during his youth confined itself to observation. It remained mere "positivism" applied to historical facts and therefore got lost in them. Like all strict positivism, it found itself unable even to account for the content that is each individual fact. There was no instance to which to apply for a decision whether such or such an event that had occurred in Attica or in Bactria actually was a religious or literary or social event. Lacking any previous distinct idea about the nature of religion as a subjective activity of man, there was no way of even taking hold of the event at issue.

In short, the Historical School was content with merely seeing, and did not proceed to effective historical thinking; it did not really produce history. And that is graver than it seems. For it might be supposed that man can do without his history. But human reality is not all actuality. God, world, state, society, art are, to be sure, problems that affect us by themselves and not merely as facts of the past; hence the science of human phenomena is not only history *sensu stricto* but also theology, philosophy or world interpretation, jurisprudence, sociology, esthetics, and so on. But once the road is blocked by which the ingenuous confidence of former days used to advance *directly* toward absolute solutions, there is no other way of setting up all those sciences, which guide human conviction and action, except as historical investigation of the ideas heretofore held about these themes.[17]

For this reason, history in its broadest sense, that is, the humanities or "sciences of man"—the sciences that have also been called moral, cultural, spiritual, and so on—are at least as indispensable as the natural sciences.

Two alternative procedures present themselves. Historical thinking may be conducted as a special case of *physical reason*, or it may be given a foundation of its own in the form of *histori-*

[17] Consequently, Dilthey's generation, empiricist as it was, tried to carry on philosophical, juridical, social investigation by means of historical *induction*. But the attempt was doomed; for there is no such thing as "inductive logic" which, under the influence of John Stuart Mill, was so widely discussed at that time.

cal reason. The first formed the aim of French and English positivism—Comte, Stuart Mill, Spencer, and so on. The second was
to be undertaken by the genius of Dilthey.

The task he set himself was a *counterpart* to Kant's enterprise.
Parallel to the *critique of pure* (that is physical) *reason,* Dilthey
proposed a *critique of historical reason.* As Kant had asked:
How is natural science possible? Dilthey asked: How is history
possible and the sciences of state, society, religion, art? His
problem was epistemological; it pertained to "critique of
knowledge." In this point Dilthey was a true son of his time.
Strictly speaking, he never succeeded in abandoning an attitude that envisages philosophical problems from the standpoint
of "theory of knowledge." He writes:

> All science is empirical; but all experience has its original connec-
> tion and its validity as determined by this connection in the condi-
> tions of our consciousness wherein it arises—in the whole of our
> nature. This standpoint, which logically entails recognition of the
> impossibility of going back behind those conditions—of seeing, as it
> were, without eyes, or of directing the ray of vision behind the eye
> itself—I will call the epistemological standpoint; modern science
> can accept no other.[18]

We seem to hear Kant, down to the details of terminology.
Nonetheless, Dilthey scents in Kant the enemy. All he shares
with Kant is the imperative, felt throughout the century, to
found all knowledge upon investigations into the conditions of
the consciousness that produces it. The decisive point, pregnant
with Dilthey's whole thought—and here we get a foretaste of
the care required in reading this style which takes pains to stress
nothing, and least of all what is most important—the decisive
point lies in the appended phrase "the whole of our nature,"
which seems a mere repetition of the Kantian idea, "the conditions of the consciousness wherein it arises." Dilthey continues:

> But then I became aware furthermore that from this standpoint
> the independence of the humanities can be accounted for so as to
> meet the needs of the Historical School. For from this standpoint our

[18] Dilthey, *op. cit.*, vol. I, p. xvii.

image of all nature proves to be a mere shadow cast by a reality hidden to us, whereas reality as it is in itself we possess only in the facts of consciousness given in inner experience. Analysis of these facts forms the core of the humanities, and thus knowledge of the principles of the spiritual [19] world remains, in agreement with the spirit of the Historical School, within the realm of that world, and the humanities form an independent system by themselves.

While finding myself in these points frequently in accord with the epistemological school of Locke, Hume, Kant, I was, on the other hand, compelled to define in a different way from theirs precisely the connection between those facts of consciousness in which I, like them, recognize the whole foundation of philosophy. Save for a few scientifically not fully developed attempts like Herder's and Wilhelm von Humboldt's, epistemology—empiristic and Kantian—has explained experience and cognition from facts belonging to the domain of perception exclusively. In the veins of the cognizing subject that Locke, Hume, and Kant constructed, there flows not red blood but the thin lymph of reason as a mere intellectual activity. But historical and psychological occupation with man in his totality has led me to ground the explanation of cognition and its concepts—such as outer world, time, substance, cause—in man himself with all his manifold powers as a willing-feeling-representing entity—although cognition seems to weave its concepts from the stuff of perceiving, representing, and thinking alone.

The method of the following attempt is therefore this: Against the background of the integral nature of man as revealed by experience and by study of language and of history, I will present all elements of present-day abstract, scientific thinking and seek their interconnection. It then appears that the most important elements of our image and knowledge of the world—as, for instance, living unity of the person, outer world, individuals outside ourselves, their living in time and their interaction—can all be explained from this integral human nature of whose real living process perception, will, and feeling form only different aspects. Not the assumption of our cognitive faculty being rigidly apriori, but only evolutionary history (*Entwicklungsgeschichte*), which starts from the totality of our condition, can answer the question we all want to lay before philosophy.[20]

[19] Read: human.
[20] Dilthey, *op. cit.*, vol. I, pp. xvii–xviii.

These words stand in the preface to Dilthey's first important philosophical work *Introduction into the Humanities,* the second volume of which was not published in his lifetime. We are in the year 1883; the author has passed the equinox of fifty; this paragraph is the first comprehensive expression he gives to his thought. Strange, indeed. But stranger still, this paragraph—so sparing, abstract, and formalistic, so without grace and as though saying nothing—is the only public expression he ever in his whole life gave to the general meaning of his work. It is the only clue that enables us to find our bearings in the rest of his publications, all so fragmentary and on seemingly disparate subjects.

Meanwhile there is no denying that the sentences quoted are far from precise. To assert that the legitimacy of empirical knowledge is grounded on the conditions of consciousness is but to repeat Kant. But then it turns out that with these same words Dilthey wants to express something entirely different from, and in a way opposed to, Kant. Namely, that the "conditions of consciousness," the groundwork of all cognition, are not only, as for Kant, conditions of intellectual consciousness— or rather, intellectual conditions of consciousness—but also conditions of will and feeling or, to quote Dilthey, "the integral nature of man." This leaves us as wise as before regarding the aforementioned discrepancy with Kant. For in Kant's philosophy, after all, will comes in through practical reason, and feeling through judgment. As it is, this one and only paragraph in Dilthey's work that deals with fundamentals does not help any to understand his philosophical intention. Had we not traveled on our own feet along the same road as Dilthey and a little beyond him, a fruitful understanding of this paragraph would prove as impossible to us as it has to all others, not his immediate pupils, who have read it during these forty years.

And yet the idea, so stammeringly expressed in these sentences, is in itself simple and lucid enough to be explained on the few pages that follow.

✳ 1. There is no other cognition than experience.[21]

2. Experience consists in perception and apprehension of facts—which, being outer or inner facts, are given in either sense perception or introspection—and in intellectual appropriation of them by means of the logical operations of comparing, distinguishing, identifying, inferring, and so on. Perception and the logical operations together may be brought under the common heading of "intellectual activities" or cognitive consciousness.

3. The intellectual activities exercised in each concrete case necessarily possess a previous generic constitution consisting in the general conditions of their exercise. For example, my now perceiving this piece of printed paper and then thinking it "as" a piece of printed paper presupposes certain general conditions of perceiving and thinking. My perception presents this piece of paper to me as an object of the outer world. The character "object of the outer world," common to all that is seen, heard, touched, is not *explicitly* perceived in any concrete case. It is an element of every concrete perception and as such a prerequisite or condition of perceiving consciousness; but precisely for this reason it does not appear *detached* and *defined* in any particular perception I have of this paper. To notice it, I must subject my perception to an analysis.

The same holds for the operation of thinking, strictly speaking. In thinking that "this before me" is a piece of printed paper, I ascribe to it, among other things, identity; it is a something determinate and distinguished from any other something including any other piece of printed paper. It may *equal* another one, but being equal does not make it the *same*. Its *selfsamehood* or identity is not visible in the piece of paper as is its color; I ascribe identity to it. That is what makes this act of mine an

[21] I should not like to make a mistake, but it seems that in Dilthey's whole work no mention is made of mathematical cognition. This much is clear: when stating the empirical character of cognition, Dilthey refers to cognition of realities. "Pure" sciences, like logic and mathematics, would therefore appear to furnish tools for cognizing rather than knowledge proper.

operation of thinking, distinguished from simply perceiving.

"Outer reality" and "identity" are therefore two elements, two prerequisites or conditions, of my consciousness of this piece of paper—that is, of my experience or knowledge of it.

4. In order to justify the validity or claim to truth inherent in experience or cognition we must therefore (*a*) find all decisive elements, prerequisites or conditions, of cognitive consciousness; (*b*) demonstrate the interconnection and unity—that is, the system, of these conditions; (*c*) ascertain how, to what degree, and in what sense this system satisfies that claim to truth.

It is in this last point that a first and fundamental discrepancy between Dilthey and his time on the one hand and Kant on the other manifests itself. Both use the same expressions but in a radically different sense.

When Kant sets out to establish the validity of experience by searching for its conditions in consciousness, what he looks for are the "conditions of the possibility of experience"—which means that he imagines or constructs apriori what our consciousness and its relation to reality *must be* like in order that the claim to truth attached to our actual experience may seem reasonable and intelligible. For Kant, the conditions of experience do not appear in experience but are pure intellectual construction and, as such, figments. The elements of consciousness—and this is characteristic of Kantianism—are not given in that consciousness whose elements they are; they are not facts of consciousness but the philosopher's hypotheses.

Dilthey's attitude, on the other hand, is empirical throughout. Experience is a reality of consciousness: I am aware that there is now a printed paper before me, and I am aware of my thinking it as printed paper with all the attributes thereby implied. Being a fact of consciousness and being given to me in immediate awareness are synonymous. Experience, knowledge, science, all science with its claim to truth are facts of consciousness. To show the legitimacy of this claim, which is an evident fact of consciousness, can consist in nothing else than in discovering the real elements or conditions of consciousness that make up experience and engender its claim before our very eyes—in discovering, therefore, not the conditions of the possibility of experience but the conditions of the reality, the actuality, of experience.

When I *in fact* claim that a thought of mine is true, this claim presents itself within me as motivated *in fact* by another *fact* of consciousness—for example, another thought of mine which I call "proof" or "reason" of the first. This proof, for its part, draws its validity from yet another fact of consciousness, and so on. All this, the initial claim as well as its justifications, is patently given in my consciousness; and so is the connection between them—namely, my awareness that I believe in this piece of thinking *because* I have previously believed in those others. Indeed, how could my claim be grounded in something that is not present in my mind and actually, *consciously,* motivating my conviction?

In tracing those chains of motivation in which my various convictions are linked together, I eventually arrive at a set of basic convictions operative in all others. For instance, all my alleged knowledge about corporeal bodies carries within itself as an ingredient the conviction that the outer world exists; that behind its varying appearances something (the substance) remains unchanged; that there is no change without a cause; and so on.

I thus arrive, through direct observation of the facts of my consciousness, at a stock of ultimate elements that interweave to form the fabric of all my concrete knowledge. And the problem of the validity of cognition boils down to finding which are the actual motives of those basic convictions.

But where shall I look for the motives of those basic convictions when they are themselves prerequisites for all others? All schools prior to Kant held them to be irreducible to one another or to any superior principle. They were the "simple ideas" of Descartes; the *semina veritatum* of the Renaissance; the "common notions" of the Stoics; Leibnitz' "principle of identity and sufficient reason"; Aristotle's substantial forms and principles of

being and knowing. They seemed to mark the furthest confines
of human thought. Upon them, all other knowledge rested,
while they themselves rested on nothing and therefore were
called *principia*—their name intimating that, like princes, they
were supreme and exempt from justifying their action. However, this presumed sovereignty of the principles or elements of
knowledge, expressed in such statements as that they are self-
evident, axiomatic truths, *per se nota*—this autonomy was,
strictly speaking, sheer autocracy.

With such procedure, science found herself in a disgraceful
situation. While she would not be satisfied to accept a fact simply as fact but proceeded at once to ask for its reason, she ac-
quiesced when it came to the principal issue, the principles, and
swallowed them whole as ultimate facts for which there was no
need to produce reasons. Empiricism, of which she felt ashamed
in her outlying domains, was admitted to her very core and
foundation.

Since Descartes, philosophy has striven with more or less
clarity of purpose to escape from so humiliating a situation.
But Kant alone tackled the problem in a thorough frontal as-
sault. His work proposed what before the Renaissance would
have seemed incongruous, nay scandalous: to give the rationale
for the principles or elements of knowledge, beginning with
mathematico-physical and metaphysical knowledge. It is this
problem, at once so bold and so simple, that lies behind his famous cryptic question: How are synthetic judgments apriori
possible? Those gnarled, forbidding words refer to nothing else
than the principles of knowledge.

Only, Kant believed that the rationale of those principles is
to be found *beyond* the actual empirical consciousness of which
we are hourly and daily aware, in a hypothetical "transcendental consciousness."

Why did Kant's predecessors fail to find the reason for those
principles, and why did Kant himself resort to looking for it in
something hypothetical—that is, in the nowhere, in utopia?
Because of a blindness born of a most inveterate prejudice.

Because of the belief that cognition forms a zone of our consciousness which, beginning and ending in itself, is shut off from the rest like a watertight compartment. I call this prejudice "intellectualism."

→ 5. Dilthey's decisive discovery consists in the realization that the facts of consciousness must be taken as they are and present themselves, any attempt to jump beyond our consciousness making no sense whatever. No reality exists that could be set over consciousness, and no chinks open in consciousness through which to espy what "in reality" happens behind it.

The most evident and obvious feature about facts of consciousness is that they always present themselves in connection with other facts of consciousness. When I believe something, I believe it *because* I hold such or such other convictions. When I want something, it is *for* this or that motive and *to* this or that end. In short, it is essential for a fact of consciousness to be given in connection, connectedness, context, interdependence with other facts of consciousness.[22] Consciousness is a compound, all ingredients of which are interlinked.

It is therefore erroneous to assume that the facts of cognitive consciousness are impermeable to those of desiring and feeling consciousness and that these latter may not intervene as *constitutive* factors in the intellectual process. Or more exactly, it is an error to assume that a desire or a feeling cannot act as motive, ground, or sufficient *reason* for a belief. Indeed, cognition *depends* on will and feeling as these depend on it. The fundamental ideas or convictions have no motive, ground, or "reason" in other convictions *because* they are grounded in volitions and sentiments. In other words, cognition cannot be explained by itself but only as a member of the integral human consciousness.[23]

[22] All these terms (and some more should be added) try to render the various shades of the word Dilthey wrote more often than any other: *Zusammenhang*.
[23] This is the second fundamental distinction between Dilthey and Kant. But with this idea, which is his exclusively, Dilthey stands alone among his contemporaries, differing not only from Kant but from the entire philosophical tradition which was *intellectualistic*. This idea of Dilthey's is not without predecessors; but dealing with them must be left for another occasion.

/Thus the principles of knowledge which seemingly formed a border admitting of no beyond and resting on no other ground or reason may be shown to derive from, and to be rooted in, other parts of our consciousness. And as those other parts—the realms of will and feeling—are in their turn based on our knowledge and convictions, it becomes clear that our consciousness forms a closed cyclical system, all parts of which find their explanation and reason within the system itself.[24] /

Epistemology would then consist in tracing the motives of the fundamental concepts through the whole organism of our mind and in giving an accurate account of the part those concepts play in the integral functioning of our mind.

If, broadening Kant's problem, we ask ourselves how the principles of all sciences—natural and historical—are possible, we become aware of the necessity of another science which must investigate the actual setup of human consciousness, that base and clue to everything else. This science—fundamental because it deals with fundamentals—will therefore start out as psychology, but a psychology planned in a way to illuminate the general structure of consciousness and the generic system of its functioning in short, the reality of *living* consciousness in its typical articulation.[25] This science will, by the same token, be the true philosophy.[26]

[24] Dilthey, it is true, never said and, in all likelihood, never clearly thought this. Nonetheless, it is what he *did* and what, therefore, was implicit in his thinking, what his thinking was. When far back in his youth—the date can be determined quite closely, thanks to excerpts published from his diary—the idea of historical reason first dawned upon him, he had not the faintest notion that his radical empiricism was to lead him with supreme simplicity to the same goal Hegel had, at the cost of endless fictions and sleights of hand, pursued with his radical logicism. Much later Dilthey *felt* this affinity. But I doubt that he saw with full clarity what it consisted in—namely, the cyclical condition of consciousness; that no act or state of consciousness is an abrupt beginning or a blind end; that they all come from something and go toward something—in one word, the strict continuity of human consciousness.

[25] Two epochs may be distinguished in Dilthey's work. In the first, he believed that the fundamental science is psychology, a psychology, however, of not quite the same type as what was currently understood by that name. In the second, convinced that he would not reach his objective in this way, he abandoned psychology and turned to what he called *Selbstbesinnung*—reflection of the subject upon himself, *autognosis*.

[26] This discipline, which is concerned with the general and invariable struc-

/In Dilthey's opinion philosophy is an empirical science; it is the last and decisive act in which man *qua* intelligence takes possession of the *whole* reality which is *his* reality, without such abstractions and specializations as are, and always were, performed by all other forms of cognition, including traditional philosophy./

How can such knowledge of human consciousness be obtained? I can observe my own mind; but that is not sufficient for knowing the mind of other people, let alone that of people of other times. Dilthey, as we have seen, is imbued with the new "historical consciousness." Like the school that bears this name, he is convinced that man cannot be defined apriori, for man's reality is pregnant with innumerable forms. Even without dwelling upon the singular character of each individual and considering generic human forms only (already an abstraction) we have primitive man, man in Chaldea and Assyria, Pharaonic man, Persians, Greeks, Romans of the Republic and the Empire, the Germans of Tacitus, the romanized Goths, and so forth and so on. Are their minds, as to structure and way of functioning, identical with mine? I can work out a psychology of myself and perhaps of my contemporaries; of all other men I have not a psychology but at best a history.

/That general science of man, that spiritual anthropology which, according to Dilthey, is philosophy will therefore have for the subject matter of its investigation the whole of human nature as revealed in "experience, study of languages and of history." "Experience" here stands for the psychology of oneself and one's contemporaries; study of language, for philology. What philology and history teach us about past man is contrasted with what psychology discloses about present man, and vice versa./

As will be noted, this philosophy, so clear in its purpose, is yet

ture of human consciousness and therefore presents itself at first in the form of psychology, is to hold, in respect of the bulk of historical facts, the same position which, in classical physics, mechanics holds in respect of observed and observable physical facts. Like mechanics, it is to play the role of a regulative discipline. History would then constitute itself in essential analogy to physics.

vague as to its method and structure. Which is to triumph in
the end, psychology over history or history over psychology?
Both are empirical; no hierarchy seems to assign a place to one
above the other. But such equality of right between psychology
and history produces a vicious circle. The science of history
must be grounded in a thorough knowledge of man; but knowledge of man must in its turn, at least partly, proceed from history.[27]

We have here arrived, however, at only the first expression of
Dilthey's thought. The next step will be to set forth the form he
gave in the second phase of his personal development to this
pivotal idea of all his work.[28]

---

[27] Dilthey later gave careful consideration to this vicious circle which persists,
however, even in the purest form of his philosophy and which he regards as
essentially inherent in cognition.

[28] The irrationality of the principles of knowledge, with which rationalism is
faced in the end, is due to the fact that reason is understood as "pure reason,"
detached and isolated. But when "pure reason" is founded on the totality of
"living reason," the irrationalism to which proud reason sees itself condemned
dissolves and turns into clear and ironical rationalism. For many years I have
therefore described my own philosophical standpoint as a *ratio-vitalism*. My
book *El tema de nuestro tiempo* (The Modern Theme), Madrid, 1923, presents
the issue of embedding pure reason in living reason as the theme of our time.
It was this that Dilthey wished to express and wished to think and in the end
failed to lay hands on. Now after the posthumous publication of his papers,
which came considerably later than the first edition of my aforementioned book,
we are able to see what was hovering before his mind. In his *Collected Writings*,
vol. VIII, p. 177 (1931), I find a remark which he was far indeed from committing to print during his lifetime and which could have stood in an old article
of mine "Ni vitalismo ni racionalismo" (Neither Vitalism Nor Rationalism),
Revista de Occidente, 1924: "What is presented to us (*das uns Gebotene*) is
actually irrational; the elements by means of which we perceive are irreducible
to one another." The remark is aimed at Hegel.

In 1924, no one in Germany, nor I from Spain, could have foreseen that this
was the *future* meaning with which Dilthey's philosophy would go down in history. The simple truth is that at that time we were, a few of us, independently
evolving the idea in the light of which Dilthey's work was to acquire fruitful
meaning. So much for his primary idea; but "living reason" signifies something
more decisive than Dilthey could have suspected.

The truth is that Dilthey was unable to free himself from the idea of vital irrationalism, as contrasted with intellectual rationalism, and did not yet discover
the new rationality of life. That explains why, toward the end of his life, he
could still write a sentence like this: "In all comprehension of life, there is an
element of irrationality, since life itself is irrational" (Dilthey, *op. cit.*, vol. VII,
p. 218).

SECOND EXPRESSION OF THE
FUNDAMENTAL IDEA

The first expression of Dilthey's idea had biographical character. In it the idea shaped itself according as Dilthey, step by step, conceived of it. First: state of "historical consciousness" or ascertainment that everything human (save for the very fact of the existence of man) is relative to a time. Second: consequent necessity of accounting for this historical consciousness as expressed in the assertion—the one that stands when all others break down—that the substance of man is relativity, historicity. Third: postulate of a science of the human phenomenon as such, a science which, *since it is the fundamental discipline* and concerned with the *one reality saved from the shipwreck*—man—must be recognized as representing what, throughout the ages, has gone under the name of philosophy.

Thirteen years later, in 1896, Dilthey was asked to write a brief summary of his philosophy for Ueberweg's history of philosophy. Nothing more understandable than that the authors of that work should have felt obliged to resort to Dilthey himself for an authentic formulation of his thought. What else could they have referred to? No more than any other contemporary philosophers could they have been expected to discern a philosophical system in the two or three paragraphs quoted above.

Dilthey set to work. Under this outward pressure—by no means trifling, for the monumental work initiated by Ueberweg exercised and is exercising an enormous influence in the philosophical world—he strove to give clear and unencumbered expression to his idea. He made various drafts—three at least.[29] Vain effort. The longest came to four or five pages and remained

[29] These notes were found among his papers and published in Dilthey, *op. cit.,* vol. VIII, pp. 174–193 (1931). Cf. also the letter to Count York of July 1896, *Briefwechsel,* pp. 219–221. That is all. By way of supplement see the study *Essence of Philosophy,* published for the first time in 1907 and again in Dilthey, *op. cit.,* vol. V, pp. 339 ff.

there, unfinished. Again this stammering genius of philosophy
chose to leave his own shrouded in silence.

Nonetheless, those attempts at formulation enable us to delineate Dilthey's final conception of what philosophy is.[30]

In what follows, we are to travel along the route of Dilthey's
idea but in the opposite direction. Instead of observing the biographical, and in this sense historical, order of the author's ar-
rival at his philosophy, we will now start from the philosophy
itself.

/ Philosophy is a human fact; and we have seen that, according
to Dilthey—herein lies his greatness and his limitation—man
has not a "nature," as the eighteenth century still believed; [31]
man has history./In Dilthey's mind this signifies various things
which he never explicitly stated and which must be enunciated
once with all rigor so as to leave no uncertainty about the meaning of this proposition.

1. Man is historical in the sense that he has no actual and
immutable constitution but assumes most varied and diverse
forms. History, in the first instance, signifies the simple fact that
the human being is variable.

2. Man is historical in the sense that what he is at each given
moment includes a past. Remembrance of what happened to
him and what he was before bears upon what he is *now*. History
here means persistence of the past, to *have* a past and to come
out of it.

3. This remembrance of the past influences our actuality
inasmuch as it furnishes a summary of our former life.[32] Re-

[30] Final, let it be noted, with respect to the general architecture of philosophical knowledge, not with respect to particulars of the doctrines that pre-
ceded Dilthey. As regards these latter, his views undergo a decisive change after
1900 from which arises the most profound and fruitful form of his thought. In
his seventies, then?

[31] In *An Enquiry Concerning Human Understanding*, Sect. VIII, Part I, 65,
Hume, though the least "rationalistic" thinker of his century, says: "It is universally acknowledged that there is a great uniformity among the actions of
men, in all nations and ages, and that human nature remains still the same, in
its principles and operations."

[32] Remembering would be impossible if the remembered piece of life were
to reappear with all its details and thus to occupy the same time it filled when it
was originally lived. Remembrance is, by itself, foreshortened life.

membering already contains a grain of interpretation. And it is precisely for this that it influences our "now." History only amplifies and purifies that explanation or *knowledge* of my life which remembering initiates. In this new signification history is the more or less adequate reconstruction which human life produces of itself.

→ 4. These three significations arising from one another interweave to form an ultimate meaning according to which history is the attempt to bring to its possible perfection the interpretation of human life by conceiving it from the viewpoint of all mankind in so far as mankind forms an actual and real unity, not an abstract ideal—in short, history in the formal sense of universal history.[33]

Nor does Dilthey trifle with the historical consistency [34] of man. He is in radical earnest about each of these four significations, considering them in the order in which they here appear.

Thus in dealing with human issues Dilthey, before deciding anything about them, looks for their various manifestations in the past—that is, treats them with rigorous historical empiricism. Nor does he change his method when the matter in hand is the human issue, philosophy. He begins the exposition of his idea of philosophy with these words:

The question: What is philosophy? cannot be answered according to personal taste. The function of philosophy can only be discovered empirically from history. To be true, the historical facts must be understood from that spiritual aliveness which continues to prevail in ourselves, making us susceptible to philosophical experience. Wherever from the store of available knowledge a synthesis arose

[33] In a more detailed study of Dilthey's idea of history, illustrations could be given from his work for each of these meanings, although the texts to be adduced would be few and far between, some of them appearing at most unexpected places.

[34] Traditional philosophy distinguishes between the *essence* and the *existence* of a thing. But the term "essence" bears various significations, which should be kept apart so as not to impair one another in more complicated cases. The obvious and least assuming signification of essence would be that a thing not only exists but also *consists* in something. What it consists in I call its *consistency* in contrast with its *existence*.

that pretended to general validity and interlinked all elements of mental life into one cognitional whole, there was philosophy. The nature of such synthesis differed according to the circumstances and always stood under the sway of the general intellectual determinants of the respective epoch. But in contrast with the attitude of special sciences philosophy always searched for a synthesis extending over the whole spiritual horizon of a time. And in contrast with religion, this synthesis always aspired to the character of general validity.

There must prevail in our consciousness conditions that are apt to produce quite regularly creations of this sort whenever the spiritual situation is favorable; otherwise such regularity could not be accounted for. The structure of the mental life produces knowledge of nature, domination of nature, economic life, law, art, and religiosity; and it unites these activities in external organization. Then consciousness operating in all these forms cannot fail to recognize its inner connectedness (*Zusammenhang*) in such manifold doings. This connectedness will comprise more and more of those activities in proportion as reflection lifts them more and more above the philosophical horizon, and it will be complete only when it includes all forms of human activity that have given rise to sciences. As man's aliveness is manifest in cognition of the world, valuation, proposing of ends, so philosophy is engaged in establishing spiritual unity among all those multiple doings. And philosophy does this because hereby only can consciousness, operative in those forms, attain to an autonomous, self-determined constitution and joyful awareness of its reality and creative power. In the economy of the spirit and of society, philosophy has the function of ever anew accomplishing this task.[35]

In defining philosophy, Dilthey, we observe, is careful to steer clear of "absolutism." Living our actual lives we feel urged to find the integral unity of all our knowledge. This unity, which is at the same time expected to explain and to order the valuations

[35] Dilthey, *op. cit.*, vol. VIII, p. 189. This translation, together with the piece quoted in the previous chapter, may serve as an example of the peculiar quality of Dilthey's style. For fairness' sake it must be observed that this paragraph forms part of a draft that was found among his papers and that what he prepared for publication himself reads smoother and clearer. However, a lack of suggestive power, a certain evasive and filmy quality of concepts and presentation, prevails throughout his work.

deriving from our feeling and the ends pursued by our will, is an immediate fact of our living consciousness,[36] and the search for it we take, for the time being, to be philosophy. It is a search that differs from all other modes of cognition in that it rises above special scientific pursuits and aspires to unite them in one whole, establishing unity, moreover, between all we know and all we feel and desire. It proceeds, therefore, by harking back from man dispersed in a variety of scientific activities to the living wholeness that man is and from which, by a process of differentiation, those several activities have evolved.

In this sense of total unification philosophy coincides with religion. But it also differs from it in that philosophical unification presents itself with a claim to validity for every man and imposes itself upon every mind by virtue of the cogency peculiar to thought. "Everywhere [37] the birth of philosophy depends, therefore, on the condition that religious conviction is no longer able to satisfy the most advanced persons. Thus symbolical conception of dogmas, allegorical interpretation of religious documents, of the doctrine of salvation, will everywhere form the background of philosophy in the making." All this marks the opening phase of philosophy, while philosophy proper signifies "fully developed autonomy of the human mind"—consciousness, that is, of living independently and not out of tradition or revelation. "And even though from the pride of knowing may spring disappointment and heartache, it is in philosophy alone that man's aspiration to free exercise of reason, hence the autonomy of the subject, can be realized." Philosophy is no mere intellectual concern; in it the totality of the subject—thought, will and feeling—aspires to autonomy.

This function, which philosophy represents, or serves, in our

[36] Let it be noted that Dilthey does not use the expression "living consciousness"; he speaks of *Seelenleben* (mental life) or, at most, of *Lebendigkeit* (aliveness). The difference, though seemingly negligible, is decisive; for it presupposes a step that Dilthey was never able to take and without which this great philosopher of "life" never succeeded in firmly establishing himself within the idea of life.

[37] Dilthey, *op. cit.*, vol. VIII, p. 190.

own lives, is discernible in one way or another in all those epochs in which life was not based exclusively on religion or myths. The doctrines embodying the respective philosophy, and even the conception of the philosophical theme and methods, have varied a good deal. Therefore any attempt to form an idea of what philosophy is through mere historical induction, by simply collating the formulas of the philosophers, would be a mistake. Such a procedure cannot but result in a zero definition, since the multiplicity of formulas produces nothing but their mutual annihilation. It can, however, teach us that history cannot be made from the past alone. The past has to be complemented by another instance—that is, ourselves.

In the analysis of our own mental life philosophy does not primarily appear as a doctrine or a formula. We arrive at these because our mental life prods us to seek them. Philosophy is a constant *function* of our living consciousness, a function which, immutable itself, produces most diverse "philosophies." Having once elucidated the working of this function of consciousness within ourselves, we can detect it in past periods and will then recognize its identity and permanence throughout the most divergent doctrines.

Two and only two, therefore, are the properties defining philosophy in its character as a permanent and identical function of human life throughout its history: totality of theme, autonomy of mode.[38] Any other definition would be too narrow and apply to special directions of philosophy only. But once the identical function of philosophy has been clearly grasped the reason for its multiform manifestations will as clearly appear.

In philosophy, man responds to the totality of the horizon that lies open to his consciousness. But the horizon varies; it would be too long to describe how and why. Confronted with

[38] For many years I have in my classes explained philosophy as the human occupation that is governed by these two imperatives: *pantonomia* and *autonomia*. However, in contrast with Dilthey, I considered and still consider those two characters as secondary. Behind them lies a more fundamental and more decisive problem which Dilthey did not see and which I hope to take up another time.

a particular horizon "the philosophy of a people or a time stresses one dimension of life from which it starts and to which it subordinates the others." That is to say, a hierarchy is forcibly established, and from it arises the philosophical doctrine that *serves*, in each case, the permanent function of philosophizing. "And in the beginning this synthesis is always posited as an objectivity, until a clearer insight reveals its seams and fissures and leads to its being reabsorbed into subjectivity." In other words, it leads to the recognition that this synthesis is not reality itself but only an inadequate and defective interpretation advanced by the subjective mind.

Philosophy is at once "an aptitude and a need" that we come upon in our own consciousness. But in order to satisfy this need and work out our own philosophy we must make use of all that lies in our consciousness; and in our consciousness there are, whether we like it or not, the results attained by the past. Our own consciousness, what we have in ourselves and what makes us, is historical. To Dilthey's generation this inexorable condition of all consciousness, to be historical, had come to be a primary evidence; Dilthey found it acting upon himself without any effort on his part. Not only was he historically conditioned, but he *knew* that he was. He had no way but to turn to the past even in the primary pursuit of defining philosophy. But awareness of one's historical condition entails another obligation, that of recognizing that the first philosophical task, and therewith the opening discipline of philosophy, consists in raising the philosophical aptitude and the philosophical need inherent in the individual to a full and concrete realization of their historical place. How can that be done? Very simply: by reconstructing "the phases of their history," "the successive attitudes adopted by the mental life of man." Thus philosophy essentially begins with being its own history. History of philosophy is "the indispensable propedeutics of systematic philosophy." [39]

[39] Here again we see Dilthey arrive, by way of a most radical empiricism, at the very positions of Hegel. Like Dilthey, Hegel lets philosophy begin with a propedeutics—*Phänomenologie des Geistes*—which proposes to guide the mind from the ingenuous belief that truth is revealed by the senses to the philosophi-

It is not only that the results of our cognitive efforts cannot be "absolute"; but it would be a crass error to assume that we can think about anything in "absolute" independence of the human past, of what has been thought, felt, desired by man in bygone millenniums. We think *with* our past and *from* the level to which our past has taken us. It is therefore the philosopher's first concern to clarify the historical situation in which he finds himself. But this historical situation is itself the consequence of previous historical situations.

The successive situations or attitudes man has passed through present themselves to Dilthey reduced to the following great phases:

1. In the beginning the earth is covered as with a vegetative carpet with a boundless variety of *primitive ideas* to which historical knowledge does not reach down.[40]

2. The first epoch of civilization known to history is marked by the priestly philosophy of the Oriental peoples laid down in the doctrine of monotheism and united with an ethico-religious technique for the guidance of life.[41]

3. Only a second generation of peoples representing the Mediterranean states and cultures succeeds in setting up philosophy on the foundation of universally valid thinking. This philosophy aligns with the sciences and breaks away from religion. Mediterranean philosophy manifested itself in three different attitudes of consciousness: (*a*) In Greek philosophy an esthetic-scientific attitude prevails. The concepts are: cosmos, conceptual mathematical order of the world, cosmic reason, *formae substantiales*. Divine reason is the principle which, for intellect and will, establishes connection between the rationality of things and human reason. (*b*) A new attitude of man toward the world must be recognized in the spirit of Rome. Here the shaping of concepts starts not from esthetic feeling or theorizing

---

cal attitude in its fullness: consciousness as dialectics. And these pedagogic grades of consciousness have their counterpart in corresponding phases of history.

[40] Let us note that at the end of the last century, when Dilthey wrote this, history had not yet joined hands with ethnology.

[41] Dilthey, *op. cit.*, vol. VIII, p. 181. What follows from here on is a more or less literal translation of Dilthey.

intellect but from will as manifest in the relations of rule, liberty, law, obligation. The outcome is the scheme of a supreme *imperium,* demarcation against this *imperium* of a zone of personal freedom, law as the rule of such demarcation, reduction of the person to a mere thing dominated by will. This will seeks the principles of its action not in profound speculations but in common sense, in *notiones communes* agreed upon by a *consensus gentium,* in the *naturalis ratio.* Thus originate historical law, conviction that legal order is inviolable, legal interpretation of the very relation between man and God. (*c*) A third attitude had been developed in the priestly religions of the Orient and was raised into a philosophy during the religious struggles in the first Christian centuries. This attitude engenders the concepts of providence, creation or emanation, man's kinship to God, salvation. It manifests itself in the shifting of the gravitational center of existence into transcendence, and in consequence of this, the real world turns into an allegory of deity and a symbol of the supernatural.

Like three great musical themes, these three philosophical attitudes of consciousness interweave to form the symphony of a universal metaphysics in the philosophy of the declining Mediterranean peoples and in the rising philosophical evolution of the new peoples of the Middle Ages—the theme of religious transcendence being, as it were, dominant.

4. Then, in the epoch of Renaissance and Reformation, the Romanic and Germanic peoples come of age. The characteristic tone of their mental constitution begins to make itself felt. Impetuosity restlessly pressing on, never sated by the sensuous moment and static existence; life as a force, sudden, spontaneous and abrupt—that is the characteristic tone of the Germanic spirit. The corresponding metaphysical consciousness is much more deeply connected with the nature of will and the metaphysical character of struggle, self-sacrifice and self-surrender. Substance here means force, energy. The Germanic spirit will therefore bring forth a new society concerned not with the relations of rule but with the free exercise of personal energy and also with the manifestation of metaphysical consciousness in human relations and the sacrifices they involve. A new art will develop in which form appears broken up through force manifesting itself in expression and motion. And even in the sciences, a dynamic tendency will come to the fore.

The new philosophy now arising is wholly distinct from meta-physics as a rational science. Its presupposition is the mechanical constitution of nature. Its problem: the relation between nature and mind. Its form: starting point in consciousness and theory of knowl-edge; foundation of the possibility of comprehending, through the sciences, the objective world; establishment of an objective system within this world. In proportion as epistemology disintegrates more and more basic concepts of this world vision, the objective system of nature is more and more transformed into space-time and cause-effect relations between natural phenomena.

From the connectedness of life itself arises the urge to extend thinking about it over the interlinked whole of the world, nay of all reality. In this most comprehensive knowledge of reality, that of life would then be encompassed as one part. But this aim proves unat-tainable. And thus the pursuit of thinking implies a contradiction and hence an element of tragedy. Critical philosophy was the first to recognize this.

5. Thenceforth the development of the mathematical sciences of nature has resulted in increasing autonomy of thinking; annihilation of any attempt to objectivate the interconnected whole of life in the form of a metaphysics; harking back—first in epistemology—of new forms of philosophy to the coherent unity of life itself.

This is the historical level on which Dilthey feels himself to be placed. He sees his philosophical task determined by the tra-jectory of all this past history, with its culmination in the situa-tion indicated above. In fact, the whole situation after Kant has served

to prepare for a philosophy of self-reflection or of life, the beginnings of which are everywhere discernible. The metaphysical nexus of the world—that ring around the modern thinker's head—grows looser and looser, while at the same time scientific research probes ever deeper into the constitution of man. Philosophy would stand in dan-ger of being deprived of its mission [42] if it were not for the slow, irrepressible growth of historical consciousness and for the unfold-

[42] For philosophy had sailed in the wake of, and let itself be absorbed by, the natural sciences, forsaking its mission to grapple with the *whole* of reality and not with only one of its aspects: the sensory or material world.

ing of the humanities, whose peculiar relation to self-awareness gives hope for a new vigorous exercise of the philosophical functions proper.

It may have been with some difficulty that the reader plowed through these paragraphs which are indeed the quintessence to which universal history can be reduced. Under their drab or abstruse appearance they contain, in my opinion, the deepest insight so far gained by historical thinking. It would be tempting to enter on an interpretation of the concrete process of human history, as Dilthey sees it, and to unfold and make patent all that is implied in this supremely compact abbreviation. However, we are here concerned only with the precipitate left by this reconstruction of all past history in the hands of a man who, around 1850, had to work out his philosophy. These are the decisive points:

1. Philosophy as metaphysics has turned out to be impossible. Why? Because metaphysics, whatever its tendency or its doctrine may be, proceeds as an "absolutism" of the intellect. The task of the intellect is to construct a world picture. This is done with the living stuff we carry in our consciousness—not, therefore, with sensual data alone but also with impulses springing from sentiment, with ends proposed by will and with all the intellectual experiments of the past with which, like it or not, we have to reckon. But all this stuff is no dead thing; it is life in perpetual change and motion. Thus the world picture constructed by the intellect as something absolute and eternal is in truth a historical pattern relative to a certain time. Metaphysics conveys not the reality of the world but a "vision of the world"—reality reflected in the living, and therefore changing, mirror that is man. In short, metaphysics is an illusion suffered by the intellect owing to its being unaware that it works not by and of itself but in the service and with the material of the entire human being—with his feeling and his will and with his intellectual tradition, whether continued or opposed.

To Dilthey, metaphysics is of the same kind with "intellectualism." But intellectualism is nothing if not that illusion which leads the individual to trust that in his intellectual doings he can begin at the beginning like a primeval, or rather an abstract and absolute, being. Whereas "the evolutionary process which is the intellect does not take place in the isolated individual; to comprehend it, additional suppositions must be made; it is a process of evolution within the human species. Mankind is the true subject in whom resides the will to knowledge." [43]

With this Dilthey means to say that the intellect cannot be defined as a *faculty* of thinking or a set of abstract forms of thinking separable from their content and therefore identical for all men of all times. My thinking already starts out with certain definite ideas, certain basic convictions, the outcome of all the intellectual efforts made by past generations up to the time in which I begin to think. Being the deepest stratum of my subjectivity, those basic convictions form the mental groundwork from which my own quest takes off. This groundwork of my intellectual personality partakes of the diffuse collective life that is the human species up to the present moment. The intellect of the individual is not individual in the sense that it is free to forge its ideas from naught; rather it is, from the outset, shaped by the heritage of the historical collectivity. That which does the thinking in me is, in this perfectly empirical and by no means mystic sense, not merely I but also the whole human past.

2. Philosophy on the historical level of the 1850's must renounce intellectualism—that is, nonhistorical construction of a world by means of pure concepts. Instead, the philosophical task consists in man's becoming aware of the fact that is he, and in thus taking possession of his immediate and not constructed reality by means of straightforward investigation into his own consciousness and that which is actually happening in it. While philosophy as metaphysics was conceptual construction of the

---

[43] Dilthey, *op. cit.*, vol. VIII, p. 176. I wish to state again that, throughout the translation here presented, Dilthey's text has not infrequently been given a somewhat fuller meaning. As for what is not text but my own comment, the reader will bear in mind what I have said before, that in this case expounding is completing.

universe, this philosophy is to be what Dilthey calls *Selbst-besinnung*—self-reflection, *autognosis*.

Reflection upon itself by consciousness is the very opposite of conceptual construction. In self-reflection, the subject takes cognizance of what is happening to him, and expresses that which is happening to him in purely descriptive terms. Here thinking is careful to add nothing to the data it comes upon, and to translate them into concepts in the most accurate manner possible.[44]

All reality having been recognized as consisting in what happens in the consciousness of man, the "science" of universal reality, or philosophy, must, after its first stage of propedeutical history, take on the form of self-reflection or *autognosis*.

Already in the phase corresponding to the first exposition of his fundamental idea, Dilthey had come upon the necessity of a systematic science of human consciousness which, I have observed, plays a role with respect to pure historical empiricism similar to that played by the mechanics of classical physics with respect to sensorial observation.[45] At that time he believed that this science could and should be called psychology, because he hoped to set it up by making radical use of the psychological method of introspection.[46]

In the second phase of his thinking, Dilthey planned, and partly finished, another exposition of his psychology. He obviously did not renounce his first belief. Yet in delineating, in

[44] It is interesting to observe that Dilthey, as early as 1895, possessed in principle the idea which, in 1901, made so grandiose an entrance upon the philosophical scene under the name of phenomenology. Dilthey, however, lacked the methodical tool that Husserl was to contribute and that alone was capable of accomplishing the task so clearly beheld by Dilthey. This instrument has enabled some thinkers of my generation to tackle the problem, from the first, on a level above that of Dilthey.

[45] The radical difference between mechanics and this science of the human mind consists in the fact that mechanics is a constructive and apriori thinking whose connection with facts is, to say the least, rather loose, whereas the science of consciousness will have to be empirical itself and to adhere strictly to facts.

[46] That is the reason why "Ideas for an Analytic and Descriptive Psychology" (1894) has come to be his most famous philosophical work and the only one to exercise influence—although, owing to a queer misunderstanding, not in philosophy but in psychology.

those drafts of 1896, the general trend of his ideas, he hesitated
to use the term psychology and replaced the traditional name
by a vague and noncommittal expression, new as the title of a
science: *Selbstbesinnung, autognosis.*[47]

The method of *autognosis* is no longer introspection, at least
not explicitly, but "analysis which examines, from the sciences
down to political life, all products and functions of humankind
in order to find their irreducible conditions in human consciousness."

/ Self-reflection therefore turns out to be analysis of the human
phenomenon as such. Dilthey doubtless saw in it a counterpart
of Galileo's work which Dilthey himself called "analysis of nature." [48] In the facts of his own consciousness, man looks for a
permanent structure, for the system of constitutive functions.
Such a system will not be a hypothesis set up for the purpose
of explaining or subsuming under a law the immediate facts
found in consciousness; it must be found in consciousness as
another fact. /

Here lies the decisive difference between Dilthey's idea and
the pseudo-empiricism and "positivism" of both English psychology from Locke onward and continental psychology from
Herbart to Wundt including even Franz Brentano.

These thinkers began their observation of mental facts with
the preconception that mental facts have certain characteristics
in common with sensory facts which provide the material of
physics. Physical facts are characterized in the first place by
presenting themselves isolated and unconnected. The visual
fact that in a certain moment the ball A touches the ball B, and
the likewise visual fact that in the next moment B, which had
been at rest, begins to move, show no connection between themselves. B's motion gives in itself no sign of being related to A's
touching B. The only link between the two facts has to do not
with them but with the subject watching them. The observer

---

[47] I have found myself compelled to coin this word in order to render somewhat adequately the term *Selbstbesinnung.*
[48] Dilthey, *op. cit.,* vol. II, p. 259.

sees them in temporal succession. Succession in time is not a visual or visible but an inner or subjective fact and as such entirely different from those two movements. That two sensorial phenomena follow each other in time contains no indication of a connection between them; they present themselves *in fact* isolated, in pure dispersion and essentially unconnected. For this reason physics involves an intellectual effort; it imaginarily *supposes* a nexus between unconnected data.

Pseudo-positivism assumes apriori that the immediate facts of consciousness, like visual facts, are *in fact* unconnected and has therefore, since Hume, set up psychology as a physical science of the mind.

But an authentic and radical positivism, resolved to accept mental facts as they are given in man's reflection on himself, finds the opposite to be true. Being aware of a volition of mine, what I first find is the unquestionable fact that I am willing something. But this resolve of mine that certain things—my "ends," since my action ends in them—must be brought about by me does not present itself as an isolated fact completed in itself. My willing something always points back for its *motive* to a value feeling that has prompted me to adopt those ends. And this valuation in its turn presents itself as founded on, or motivated by, my perceptions and ideas of things. So that in the mind, in contrast with the world given by the senses, no fact stands *in fact* by itself; as much a fact, as evident and primary as a mental fact itself, is its connection with other facts.

This observation is of supreme importance. It signifies that the fundamental fact of immediate consciousness is its interconnectedness. The mind is a coherent whole; all that is in it appears interwoven, articulated, related. Relation, connectedness, integral and organic unity are the distinguishing features of the mental world taken as a pure and simple fact. In the life of the mind, the whole is prior to the parts. And since it is the relation and connection between elements that bestow "meaning" upon them, radical positivism leads to the insight that, whereas in physics it is the thinker who attaches to the naked facts a "meaning," which in themselves they have not, the very reality of mental facts is, of its own account, endowed with "meaning." Investigation of consciousness yields at the same time the facts and their explanation, the phenomena and the law. Physical laws are dictated to material bodies by the physicist; the laws of mental or spiritual life are dictated to the philosopher by this life itself.

<u>Self-reflection</u> or *autognosis* reveals that what is given in consciousness is, first and foremost, integral connectedness and organic unity of all thinking, feeling, and desiring. At the same time, self-reflection reveals that this connected unity is the ultimate reality that can be reached. "*Consciousness cannot go behind itself.*"[49] Whatever we propose to think forms part of this organic unity of our mind and is a result or consequence of it. There is no means of jumping beyond consciousness, and any attempt to explain with the help of any other imaginary system the radical connectedness in which we live and that is our mind would be absurd. Our mind is the very presupposition of all explanation. For to explain a phenomenon means, in the last instance, to point out its place and its part within the living economy of consciousness, and to determine the "meaning" it has in the original source of all meaning: life.

It is the task of philosophy as *autognosis* or man's reflection upon himself to elucidate the generic texture of the living articulation of functions which is consciousness—Dilthey calls this texture *Seelenstruktur* (structure of the mind).

How to go about it? With a twofold method: analyzing on the one hand the activities of the mind as embodied in external products—the sciences of nature, of history, of state, of society; and art, religion, politics, industry—and through such analysis reducing this immense phenomenology to certain ultimate elements; analyzing on the other hand one's own consciousness as it functions in its living totality. This analysis will serve to discover the actual unity of all these elements and will thus correct the deceptive perspective in which they appear isolated, each

[49] *Ibid.*, vol. V, p. 194.

laying claim to an independent meaning of its own. Natural science, law, state, art, economy when they stand by themselves are mere abstractions performed by our thinking upon the actual reality in which they are inseparable.[50]

To carry out this program means nothing else than setting down a theory of knowledge—knowledge of nature as well as of moral or properly human matters. But it means at the same time evolving a theory of valuation or realm of feeling and a theory of adoption of ends or realm of will.

Here we have the substantive part of philosophy: theory of knowledge. Let us note without further comment that this conception of Dilthey's contains a strange inconsistency. Critical philosophy had demonstrated before him that metaphysical objects have no reality, but man's consciousness has. The science that studies the facts of consciousness would therefore seem to be directly occupied with reality—the reality that is left, the only reality that exists. This science ought to have ontological character and to constitute, if, strictly speaking, not a science of being as being, indeed a science of *what is*. But Dilthey, a true son of his time, takes all philosophical endeavor to be directly concerned with sciences, "culture," and so on, and only indirectly and through this with reality. Thus without any intrinsic justification, self-reflection which ought to be the science of the reality "man" turns for him into a theory of the cognitive efforts performed by man. This *idée fixe* of his time hinders him from reaching his full stature. His great intuition of "mental life" as the fundamental reality remains forever mute; his thinking cannot grasp it, hampered as he is by the epistemological mania, that Kantian and positivist *ontophobia*.

As a further toll exacted by his time, we must regard Dilthey's idea of a third constitutive task of philosophy. Sciences, apart from what they are as modes of knowing, have a content. But in their dispersed state of existence, their content—and there-

---

[50] Dilthey's last somewhat different view about this methodological point, since it does not bear on the general line of his philosophy, need not be discussed here.

fore our valid ideas about the world—does not attain unity. To
establish unity, the scientific ideas must be systematized in an
"encyclopedia of the sciences"—a notion, common to those minor thinkers who, notwithstanding their being such, dominated
the European mind around 1895—Wundt, for example, that
formidable philosophical cobbler.

Let us conclude by adding the fourth and last mission incumbent, according to Dilthey, upon philosophy.

That urge toward the absolute which prompts man to erect
philosophical systems of the universe is in itself no error. The
error comes in when he trusts he can do this. But even after
having satisfied himself that he cannot, man will go on to imagine the absolute. For this yearning is an essential function of his
mind. That is to say, the "systems," degraded as regards their
claim to truth, persist and always will persist as a constitutive
fact of human consciousness. As such, Dilthey calls them "visions of the world," "images or ideas of the universe." These
world visions can be subjected to historical study; this philosophy does in its historical propedeutics, its opening discipline.
But then there arises the additional question whether history
brings forth an unlimited crop of ever-new world images, or
whether they may all be subsumed under certain ultimate recurrent types. In the latter case, all mankind would fall into
definite groups as though doomed to move perpetually within
a fixed repertory of radical modes of seeing the universe. It is
this question that gives rise to the fourth and last component of
philosophy: the theory of world visions and their classification
in types.

We then have these four themes which, according to Dilthey,
integrate philosophy:

1. History of the philosophical evolution as a propedeutics.
2. Theory of knowledge.
3. Encyclopedia of the sciences.
4. Theory of world visions.

EUROPEAN HISTORY TITLES IN
NORTON PAPERBOUND EDITIONS

Menéndez Pidal, Ramón. *The Spaniards in Their History.* N353

Newhouse, John. *Collision in Brussels: The Common Market Crisis of 30 June 1965.*

Nichols, J. Alden. *Germany After Bismarck: The Caprivi Era, 1890-1894.* N463

Pirenne, Henri. *Early Democracies in the Low Countries.* N565

Rowse, A. L. *Appeasement.* N139

Russell, Bertrand. *Freedom versus Organization: 1814-1914.* N136

Sontag, Raymond J. *Germany and England: Background of Conflict, 1848-1894.* N180

Stansky, Peter and William Abrahams. *Journey to the Frontier: Two Roads to the Spanish Civil War.* N509

Talmon, J. L. *The Origins of Totalitarian Democracy.* N510

Taylor, A. J. P. *Germany's First Bid for Colonies, 1884-1885.* N530

Thompson, J. M. *Louis Napoleon and the Second Empire.* N403

Tucker, Robert C. *The Marxian Revolutionary Idea.* N539

Waite, Robert G. L. *Vanguard of Nazism: The Free Corps Movement in Postwar Germany, 1918-1923.* N181

Wheeler-Bennett, John W. *Brest-Litovsk: The Forgotten Peace, March 1918.* N576

Whyte, A. J. *The Evolution of Modern Italy.* N298

Wolfers, Arnold. *Britain and France between Two Wars.* N343

Wolf, John B. *Louis XIV.*

Wolff, Robert Lee. *The Balkans in Our Time.* N305

Zeldin, Theodore. *The Political System of Napoleon III.* N580

THE NORTON HISTORY OF
MODERN EUROPE

Rice, Eugene F., Jr. *The Foundations of Early Modern Europe, 1460-1559*

Dunn, Richard S. *The Age of Religious Wars, 1559-1689*

Krieger, Leonard. *Kings and Philosophers, 1689-1789*

Breunig, Charles. *The Age of Revolution and Reaction, 1789-1850*

Rich, Norman. *The Age of Nationalism and Reform, 1850-1890*

Gilbert, Felix. *The End of the European Era, 1890 to the Present*

James Morton Smith, Ed.   *Seventeenth-Century America*   N629

Paul H. Smith   *Loyalists and Redcoats: A Study in British Revolutionary Policy*   N628

John W. Spanier   *The Truman-MacArthur Controversy and the Korean War*   N279

Julia Cherry Spruill   *Women's Life and Work in the Southern Colonies*   N662

Ralph Stone   *The Irreconcilables: The Fight Against the League of Nations*   N671

Ida M. Tarbell   *History of the Standard Oil Company* (David Chalmers, Ed.)   N496

George Brown Tindall   *The Disruption of the Solid South*   N663

Frederick B. Tolles   *Meeting House and Counting House*   N211

Arthur B. Tourtellot   *Lexington and Concord*   N194

Frederick Jackson Turner   *The United States 1830–1850*   N308

Harris Gaylord Warren   *Herbert Hoover and the Great Depression*   N394

Wilcomb E. Washburn   *The Governor and the Rebel: A History of Bacon's Rebellion in Virginia*   N645

John D. Weaver   *The Brownsville Raid*   N695

Arthur P. Whitaker   *The United States and the Independence of Latin America*   N271

Ola Elizabeth Winslow   *Meetinghouse Hill, 1630–1783*   N632

Bryce Wood   *The Making of the Good Neighbor Policy*   N401

Gordon S. Wood   *The Creation of the American Republic, 1776–1787*   N644

Benjamin Fletcher Wright   *Consensus and Continuity, 1776–1787*   N402

Howard Zinn   *LaGuardia in Congress*   N488

Hiller B. Zobel   *The Boston Massacre*   N606